OLD TRAFFORD

Old Trafford

JOHN MARSHALL

SPORTSMANS BOOK CLUB
Newton Abbot 1973

ACKNOWLEDGEMENTS

For generous help in research for *Old Trafford* I would like to thank, in particular, Mr J. B. Wood, Secretary of the Lancashire County Cricket Club, Mr J. D. Bond, the Lancashire captain, Mr C. S. Rhoades, Chairman of the Committee, Mr N. Oldfield, the Lancashire coach, and Mr M. Taylor, the Lancashire scorer. I am indebted, too, to cricketers past and present who have helped with their recollections. I also wish to acknowledge the following valuable sources: *Lancashire County Cricket, 1864–1953* by A. W. Ledbrooke; *Fifty Years' Cricket Reminiscences of a Non-Player* by W. E. Howard; *Lancashire* by Rex Pogson; *Lancashire County Cricket Club Centenary Brochure*; *Cricket Triumphs and Troubles* by Cecil Parkin; *The Wars of the Roses* by A. A. Thomson; *The Watney Book of Test Match Grounds* by I. A. R. Peebles; *Forty Seasons of First Class Cricket* by R. G. Barlow; *Second Innings* by T. C. F. Prittie and John Kay; *Cricket Merry-Go-Round* by Brian Statham; *Cricket all the Year* and *Good Days* by Sir Neville Cardus; *Best Cricket Stories* edited by Denzil Batchelor; *Jackson's Year* by Alan Gibson; *The History of Cricket* by Eric Parker; *Cricket, Gone to the Test Match* and *Vintage Summer, 1947* by John Arlott, *A History of Cricket*, by H. S. Altham and E. W. Swanton; and, last but by no means least, *Wisden Cricketers' Almanac*.

CONTENTS

ACKNOWLEDGEMENTS

The author's thanks are due to the following for the photographs reproduced in this book:

The Mansell Collection: 2, 5.
Central Press Photos Ltd.: 7, 8, 9, 10, 11, 12, 13, 14, 17.
Sport & General Press Agency Ltd.: 15, 16, 18.

ILLUSTRATIONS

1 *Ground With An Air*

To use a venerable guide book term, the 'environs' of Old Trafford
tend to lack aesthetic appeal, and normally fail to excite the
imagination of the artist. Yet there is about Old Trafford an air, an
unmistakeable if intangible atmosphere of tolerant friendliness
which is not fully dispelled, however desolate the climatic conditions or dastardly the intentions of invaders from across the
Pennines or the world. Perhaps the name has something to do with
it. 'Old', as in 'Old Bill' and 'Old Everlasting' has an affectionate
ring about it, suggesting avuncular benevolence and unswerving
dependability. Trafford, to be sure, has an aristocratic aura, as
have the 'environs', Warwick Road, Talbot Road, Seymour Place
—however plebeian their appearance. Indeed the links between
Old Trafford and the de Traffords have been long and strong. Sir
Humphrey de Trafford, Bart., the 'landlord' was President of the
Lancashire County Cricket Club for six years from 1881 and Sir
Humphrey Francis de Trafford for the following six years.

A de Trafford, in fact, played for the county at Old Trafford—
alas, without the distinction the family have borne through the
years. He appeared for Lancashire once in 1884 and the records
starkly proclaim his runs as 0, his highest score as 0 and his
average as 0·00. There, but for the grace of God . . .

A. Seymour's record was more glowing. His single appearance
in 1869 reaped him and posterity 45 runs, a highest score of 25
and an average of 22·50. The Warwicks are not represented, which
is scarcely surprising considering that the Earl known as the King
Maker fought on the Yorkist side in the original Wars of the
Roses. Nor are the Talbots, immortalised, let us hope for ever, in
a Bordeaux château yielding a claret as trustworthy and benign as
Old Trafford itself. But their illustrious names are on innumerable
lips each summer as the faithful journey by train to Warwick road
station or by road to the Talbot road main entrance from 'the

town' which was in Roman days Mancunium and now is thrusting Manchester.

The 'town', certainly, for the 'City' can only mean to loyal Mancunians Manchester City Football Club, which, with its equally venerated rival 'United' so worthily upholds the great sporting traditions of the industrial north west. The 'town' is justly proud of its 'local' teams which include, let there be no mistake about it, those which represent the Lancashire County Cricket Club. For the Lancashire sides stemmed from those of Manchester, and the Manchester Cricket Club it was which identified itself with Old Trafford before the county club was formed. The Manchester Club was respected and flourishing in the early years of the nineteenth century, though not at Old Trafford—the first grounds were, successively, at The Crescent, Salford, and Moss Lane, Hulme.

In 1818 the Manchester Club was formed, or reformed, under the Presidency of Mr J. Rowlandson, who was also Treasurer and Secretary. There is an early (1826) record of a match between Manchester and the Garrison, warriors from the Coldstream Guards and the Queens Bays turning out for the latter. The contest was notable mainly for the fact that one batsman was given out f.b.w—foot before wicket.

A visit to London in 1842 was not a resounding success. The Mancunians, still clinging to underarm bowling despite the round-arm revolution of the late '20s, were routed by the palpably amused Gentlemen of the M.C.C. Undismayed, or perhaps inspired, Manchester marched on, varying unrelenting rivalry with the Boughton Club (rather like that which exists between City and United today) with more exalted engagements such as that with All-Yorkshire—who returned home licking painful wounds—and an all-England team which included the formidable George Parr, from Nottinghamshire, respectfully referred to as 'the Lion of the North' and also (becoming, like Old Trafford, an esteemed institution) as 'Old George Parr'. Against Manchester he notched 64 which was modest compared with his majestic century at Leicester. The Manchester Club members, now full of confidence and looking to the future, moved to Old Trafford and, upon their fine new ground, a Lancashire team was mobilised to play Yorkshire, one of three such fixtures in the mid-nineteenth century not recognised as truly 'county matches' in the Lancashire annals.

Just as Lord's was moved from its original site, so was Old Trafford. After a gallant but forlorn battle against eviction, to make way for an Art Treasures Palace, the Club found a new ground nearby—'to the West of the great Exhibition'—about eight acres in extent and part of the ground today. The first match on this new Old Trafford ground was, appropriately enough, between Manchester and Liverpool, the railway linking the two cities which had been opened a quarter of a century earlier by the triumphant Duke of Wellington enabling staunch Liverpudlians to speed to the support of their side.

The match took place on June 10th and 11th and resulted in a win for Manchester by 31 runs in spite of the fact that their second innings realised only 46. For Manchester A. B. Rowley, member of a family closely identified with Old Trafford in its early years, took eleven wickets, ten of them bowled. It was a splendid start, justifying the faith of those who had supported the move, though it cost £1,100. It was a barely supportable burden then, but what a puny price it seems when one contemplates the lush green turf, as luxuriant as a stately home croquet lawn, the aldermanically substantial pavilion, the many stands, spacious bars and elegant banqueting suites which are Old Trafford in the 1970s. The site of Old Trafford Number One may still be fixed by the earnest explorer. Depending upon his interests it progressed/degenerated via Botanical Gardens to a greyhound track.

Not that our Old Trafford was ungracious in its infancy. The Pavilion was described, at the time of the ground's opening, as 'a great ornament to the ground'. It even possessed a wine cellar fit for gourmets. Six years later the news that Yorkshire had formed a county cricket club caused some consternation in the Manchester ranks. Why hadn't they thought of it first? Zealous Manchester cricketers wasted little time. In January 1864, a meeting was called to consider the propriety of forming a county cricket club. It was attended, according to a contemporary report, by amateur cricketers from all over the county; they decided in favour. It was an historic decision in an historic year. Two of cricket's great institutions both made their debuts, W.G., whose first two innings in first class cricket, at the age of 15, brought him 5 and 38 runs, and the 'cricketer's bible', *Wisden*, a slender, diffident first edition worth a large sum today. The year was also notable, in London, for the formation of the Middlesex County Cricket Club and in

Manchester, not only for the launching of Lancashire C.C.C., but for the founding of the Wholesale Co-operative Society.

Though the original object of the new county club was to hold matches alternately in Manchester, Preston, Blackburn and other venues, Old Trafford was, virtually from the start, the county club's home.

The first match played by the Lancashire club, however, took place not at Old Trafford, but at Warrington, and the opponents of the county side, all amateurs, including two of those Manchester stalwarts, the Rowleys, were not another county but Birkenhead Park and Ground. Face was saved only by the clock. There followed a return match which was honourably drawn, the county being reinforced by professionals, and games against the Gentlemen of Shropshire, Warwickshire and Yorkshire.

Lancashire's first inter-county match at Old Trafford was played on July 20th, 21st and 22nd, 1865. Those other new boys, Middlesex, were the visitors, a fine game it was throughout and, happily for the northern county's records, the Londoners were beaten by 62 runs despite the outstanding feats of the Walkers of Southgate. It was, indeed, a game full of interest watched by such a small gathering that the gate amounted to a miserable £25. Lancashire batted first and scored 243 runs. All but two of the Lancastrians reached double figures. Middlesex then proceeded to compile precisely the same total, thanks mainly to R. D. Walker, who hit 84, and opener A. J. Wilkinson, who scored 59. Lancashire's second innings of 178 provided V. E. Walker with the bowler's dream, all ten wickets, R. D. Walker helping by holding two catches off his unpredictable lobs, one of which disposed of A. B. Rowley, top Lancashire scorer with 60 after 24 in the first innings. Middlesex then crumpled, only the Walkers offering real resistance with 29 and 28 out of a total of 116.

The main destroyer was Roger Iddison, a professional not only playing for Yorkshire but captain of the Yorkshire team! He took five wickets, having already claimed three in the Middlesex first innings. Fellow professional Fred Reynolds had six wickets in the match so that the core of this memorable contest might be said to have been the Northern pros v the Southern (or Southgate) amateurs. Qualification to play for a county—other than Yorkshire, which insisted from the start upon sons of its own soil only— was at this stage a haphazard affair. Yorkshire's Iddison—who played for that county from 1855 to 1876, scoring more than 2,000 runs and taking over 100 wickets and was captain from the formation of the Yorkshire C.C.C. in 1863 until J. Rowbotham took over in 1871—actually hit the first century ever scored for Lancashire. That was in 1868 against Surrey at the Oval. It was an invaluable knock, for Lancashire had followed on, Surrey having amassed quite the biggest score against them up to that point in history, 422. Lancashire, in fact, wrought revenge the following year, running up 429 on the same ground, due largely to a remarkable innings of 195 by a professional named James Ricketts, playing in his first county game. Going in number one, he carried his bat and, altogether, it was a feat which has no parallel. Ricketts was in and out of the side for a decade but failed to live up to this spectacular promise; in fact his aggregate only just topped 1,000 runs in those ten years, his average being 17·20.

Iddison, ironically, had a better average for Lancashire as a batsman, 23·88, than for Yorkshire, 19·00. For Lancashire he took 56 wickets at an average cost of 15·62 runs, for Yorkshire 109 at 15·47 each. Yorkshiremen, it would seem, have always been welcome among the Lancashire fraternity at Old Trafford. When the new ground was opened in 1857 a house was provided for the club's professional bowler, Thomas Hunt, a Yorkshireman who first played for that county in 1845. He died at the age of 39 before the Lancashire club was formed and a benefit match was played to help his widow—the first benefit match recorded at Old Trafford. The next benefit to be found in the annals was accorded in 1870 to Fred Reynolds, who was much more than a playing professional. He was, at Old Trafford, the general factotum, managing the cricket, collecting subscriptions, looking after the ground and looking after the members too. His salary was £60 a year but he had a rent free cottage and the privilege of shooting pigeons, a 'perk' which brought him into conflict with the Committee when he invited friends who were non-members to join him in a shoot.

County matches on the ground, used by Lancashire only by permission of the Manchester Club, were not numerous in the county club's early years, but they were varied and attractive. Surrey, Nottinghamshire, Sussex, Hampshire, Derbyshire and Kent were all opponents, but Middlesex vanished from the fixture list after 1868 and did not reappear for fifteen years.

The first 'Colonial' team ever to visit us, the Australian

Aboriginals with their quaint names, 'Tiger', 'Redcap', 'Dick-a-Dick', 'Twopenny and 'King Cole', and their after-match boomerang throwing displays, provided a diversion in 1867 when the first of the endless 'roses battles' (discounting the two preliminary skirmishes in 1849) were waged. There were, in fact, three matches between Lancashire and Yorkshire, the first of all involving properly constituted county clubs, opening at Whalley on June 20th. It was won by Yorkshire, as were the matches at Old Trafford and Middlesbrough. So keen was the red rose-white rose rivalry, indeed, that a fourth game, involving the Gentlemen of Lancashire and the Gentlemen of Yorkshire was also played that season.

The third of the 'proper' county matches between the two rivals was significant for the first appearance in the Lancashire team of that illustrious, commanding and heroic all-round exemplar, Arthur Neilson Hornby, of Blackburn. He had played previously with his brother E. K. for the Gentlemen of Lancashire versus the Gentlemen of Yorkshire and (such was the tolerance of Lancastrians in the matter of representation) with three of his brothers, for the Gentlemen of Cheshire *against* the Gentlemen of Lancashire. Young Mr Hornby's contributions in the Middlesbrough match were not spectacular, 2 runs and 3 runs, but he was soon to display the tenacity of purpose and all-round prowess which had assured him of immortality in an Eton-Harrow match at Lord's, where jubilant Harrovians had carried him to the pavilion after he had personally ensured victory over Eton with his bat. At that time he was diminutive, weighed less than six stone and was, in consequence of his wiry lack of flesh rather than any sharp resemblance, known as 'monkey' Hornby. Few cricketers have evinced his vast enthusiasm for the game, his total dedication.

At Oxford University he was dismayed to discover that he was expected to study as well as play cricket so he hastened to join the family's milling business in his native Blackburn, a thriving concern which he was in some danger of demoralising so often did he lure the staff on to his beloved cricket fields. There was relief, therefore, when he directed his devotion to Old Trafford, playing under the captaincy of Edmund Rowley until he took over the post in 1880, rapidly to establish a reputation as the toughest and most completely authoritarian of all county captains with the possible exception of his autocratic and aristocratic rival, Lord Hawke across the border.

Hornby was the first of many great Lancashire cricketers to be remembered as a personality as well as a performer. Certainly there had been some good players in those largely amateur early county sides supported so enthusiastically by the Rowley family, just as later teams were to be identified with the Steels and the Hornbys. William Hickton, for example, like so many others a 'foreigner', from Derbyshire—he was a fast, roundarm bowler of considerable menace.

In 1867 at Lord's he took eleven M.C.C. wickets for 91 runs, Lancashire losing a rain-soaked match—mops were used to soak up the puddles on the pitch—by 50 runs. Three years later he achieved fame with 'all ten' against Hampshire at Old Trafford. His match record was 14 wickets for 73 runs.

Behind the wicket in the Lord's match was Gideon Holgate who, like Iddison, showed a fair impartiality by playing as well for Yorkshire, his native county. But a Lancashire man born and bred, at Preston, Cornelius Coward, noted for his wristy cutting, provided some batting backbone in the county's first encounters. Perhaps his most notable performance was a determined innings of 85 against Middlesex in 1866, after Lancashire had lost five batsmen for 16 runs. These early Lancashire professionals, though fewer in numbers than the amateurs, certainly pulled their weight.

The amateurs included some outstanding cricketers who were apt to dazzle in the all-amateur matches which remained a feature of the fixture lists. E. B. Rowley, for the Gentlemen of Lancashire against the Gentlemen of Yorkshire hit 219, a very tall score in 1867. He also had the awesome distinction of being the first player ever to hit a ball clean out of Old Trafford from a wicket in its middle. The first century by an amateur in the county side was recorded by the Rev. Frank Wynyard Wright, from Oxfordshire, 120 not out against Sussex, to which county he subsequently emigrated, teaching at Eastbourne. He had been an outstanding boy cricketer at Rossall School. Unfortunately for Lancashire, he played in only 14 matches for them, with the very useful average for those days of 22·61.

In 1871 an event of much subsequent significance passed almost unnoticed. R. G. Barlow took a wicket with his first ball in county cricket, against Yorkshire of all opponents. Yet for a long time he was regarded as chiefly a batsman. Indeed, with Alec Watson, William McIntyre and Arthur Appleby in the team he did not have a chance to bowl. McIntyre, in 1872, took 41 wickets averaging under 6 runs each, Watson had 20 and Appleby 12. All opposing batsmen not accounted for by these three were run out. But Barlow could scarcely complain. The team won all their four county matches.

2 *Oh, My Hornby and My Barlow*

Like many of cricket's great pairs—Brown and Tunnicliffe, Gilligan and Tate, Hendren and Hearne, Hobbs and Sutcliffe, Makepeace and Hallows, Trueman and Statham—Arthur Nielson ('Monkey', later 'Boss') Hornby from Blackburn, and Richard ('Dicky') Barlow, from Barrow Bridge, Bolton, were contrasting in many ways. Hornby, an amateur and a born leader, was as dashing as professonal Barlow was cautious—a stonewaller with some astonishing endurance performances among his records. Hornby was small, wiry, military even to the authoritative moustache, mercurial. Barlow, solid, stolid, clearly belonged to the 'other ranks'. Francis Thomson, in the most evocative poem yet written (in crude modern idiom a proper tear-jerker), conjuring the ghosts of the past, wrote of . . . 'the run stealers flitting to and fro, to and fro,

'Oh, my Hornby and my Barlow long ago'.
But there was only one run-stealer, Hornby. And Barlow was sometimes the victim of his partner's impetuosity. Indeed the very first time they opened the innings together, in 1873, Barlow was run out for 0. Though he knew his place, Dicky Barlow was by no means inarticulate off the field among his brother professionals. Long after this initial set-back he said of Hornby—with a wry mixture of despair and admiration—'First he runs you out of breath, then he runs you out, then he gives you a sovereign'. However dour he could be at the wicket he would certainly unbend away from it; and when rain stopped play, just as frequently then as it does now, he would lead the time-beguiling sing-song. And dour he could be out in the middle. Barlow's more defensive efforts are part of cricket history, 17 in 135 minutes v Yorkshire, carrying his bat for 26 in 2 hours ten minutes against Kent, for 34 in $3\frac{3}{4}$ against Notts, and for 5 runs (out of a total of 69) in $2\frac{1}{2}$ hours, against a great Notts. This tenacity was not only inspiring or infuriating, according to the occasion, but often decisive. His

unrelenting forward defence, the bat moving massively to the ball, could and sometimes did win the day for Lancashire or for England. He was, too, a fair bowler, left-hand medium slow and devastatingly accurate. He opened both the batting and the bowling for England in one Test match, a record unique. Three times he accomplished the hat trick, including a truly startling feat for the Players, in 1884, when his trio of victims were W.G., John Shuter and Walter Read. Three years earlier he had taken 6 Derby wickets for 3 runs. Fifty times in his cricketing life he carried his bat, eleven times for Lancashire, easily a record (Hallows comes next in the list, with six). In 20 years, from 1871, Barlow played in 246 matches for Lancashire, collecting 7,687 runs and taking 726 wickets. He played in 17 Tests against Australia, hitting 591 runs and taking 35 wickets.

At the end of one of these Tests, against Australia at Old Trafford in 1886, the full score was printed on satin and presented to Barlow (with £5). This treasured memento he reproduced in his autobiography *Forty-two Seasons of First-class Cricket*. Beneath it is the sentence: 'Presented to R. G. Barlow for his very fine Batting and Bowling.' The writing is Barlow's, but this unabashed piece of self-appreciation was justified. Barlow took only one wicket in Australia's first innings, but in the second he had a remarkable analysis: 52 runs, 31 maidens, 44 runs, 7 wickets. He was second highest scorer in England's first innings with 33 not out, and defied Spofforth's expresses in the second to score 30 in an easy England victory by 4 wickets.

Such was his devotion to the game that, when he retired to Lytham in 1891, he took with him all his accumulated cricket equipment and relics, creating what was virtually a museum of cricketana in his own home. He was, in his cricket gear, the centre-piece in a stained glass window he had made for himself; his ornaments had one motif, and bats were everywhere, even in the bathroom.

Hornby, whose first-class playing days spanned 32 years, hit more than 10,000 runs for Lancashire, but his batting average was, in fact, only $3\frac{1}{2}$ runs an innings higher than Barlow's. His zest was unlimited, his determination steely; he was intolerant of inefficiency and grumbling. He set a frighteningly high standard in the field, where he was utterly fearless. He was contrary, at times cantankerous, often an awkward little cuss. He would place a player in a fielding position he knew he did not like, presumably in the interest of discipline. This fate befell the young Archie MacLaren when he had school success behind him and everything else before him. Cheekily, perhaps, he asked to be put anywhere but point. He fielded at point for a long time. W. B. Stoddart asked to be excused fielding in the deep; he was promptly sent there. Hornby was tough, imperious as captain, yet off the field he would mix easily and naturally with amateurs and pros alike. He imposed strict self-discipline upon himself and demanded it from others.

That included practice before the start of the day's play. Once he asked two of his team, Arthur Paul and James Hallows, if they had had their work-out. They confessed that they had not. The skipper then revealed that he had seen them in the bar and ordered them to pad up and open the innings. Their response was 250 runs before the first wicket fell. Yet he was often quixotically generous. Not only Barlow, his partner, was rewarded; he astounded an opposing fielder who had just got him out with a spectacular catch in the deep by giving him a sovereign.

Hornby was indirectly responsible for a significant cricket milestone, the introduction of boundaries. Before then the batsmen ran until the ball was returned. He was in the long field one day when the ball was lustily driven into the crowd. Hornby dashed after it with his usual explosive energy, scattering the spectators left and right; one was quite badly hurt. After that incident boundary lines were introduced, then fences.

Hornby was a prodigious athlete. He played rugby football for England nine times, the first when he was nearly thirty. He was a hurdler and a boxer good enough to take on some pretty ferocious prizefighters in their booths. He was contemptuous of pampering. In his latter years when he went to a football match as a spectator he expressed astonishment' as a trainer ran on to the field with towel and water to revive a player. 'What the hell does that chap want on the field?' he demanded. When told the man was injured he exploded. 'We had to attend to our own in my days,' he growled. He never wore a cap on the cricket field, probably regarding it as effete. He was, perhaps, the most dedicated cricketer of all time. He carried *Wisden* in his bag wherever he went. After his playing days he travelled, with some reluctance, to Scotland for a three weeks holiday during the season. He demanded that wires be sent to him twice a day when Lancashire were playing at Old Trafford, and a full account of the game prepared each evening. At the end of a week he was on the ground himself. He had returned for a couple of days to see a friend bat!

What cannot be doubted is that Hornby and Barlow imparted a shining lustre to Lancashire cricket in the 1870s as did W. G. Grace and his two brothers to Gloucestershire. It is therefore scarcely surprising that when these two counties met at Old Trafford in 1878 with the three Graces in the Gloucester side the crowds were so great and determined to see the game that riots broke out that made the 'demos' of the present decade look like the pranks of nicely nurtured children. On the last day of the match sods of the precious Old Trafford turf were wrenched out of the ground and hurled about as about 18,000 spectators and would-be spectators—some 2,000 had rushed the turnstiles and got into the already full ground free—milled around demonstrating their dissatisfaction with the arrangements, which were certainly in-adequate for such an invasion. Farm wagons and drays were not regarded by the proud Lancashire supporters as ideal grandstands for such an occasion. At the height of the mêlée, A. N. Hornby, though not yet then the Lancashire captain, took matters into his capable hands and attempted, single handed, to restore law and order. He galloped into the fray as if pursuing the ball, and emerged from it grasping one of the most violent agitators, handing his captive over to a policeman after he had, according to contem-porary report, administered to him 'a number of hard knocks'. There were further delays while protesting spectators were assisted from the playing area.

However the match, in retrospect, did much for Lancashire's cricket prestige and, immediately, for its finances. The gate realised £750, a gratifying sum at that moment in cricket time. And the spectators had no grounds to regret their outlay. My Hornby and my Barlow put on 108 for the first wicket in the second innings, Hornby proceeding to score exactly 100. A. G. Steel, a more than promising new all-rounder from Cambridge University, who had hit 87 against Sussex in his first county match the previous year, took 9 wickets and, in fact, the result of the game hung largely on the duel between Steel and not-so-young W.G. The latter, not for the first or the last time in his unique career, emerged the victor, his 58 not out ensuring a draw, with Gloucester still needing 111 runs with 5 wickets in hand when stumps were drawn. The vast crowd, all ugly scenes forgotten, rose to the Doctor, who had also hit 32 in the first innings and taken 4 wickets. This was, surely, the match which inspired Francis Thomson's lament. He was then, fresh from his native Preston, a medical student at Manchester, and had formed a deep affection for Old Trafford, to which he repaired whenever his studies permitted. Shortly before he died, at the age of 47, in 1907, he was asked to go to Lord's to see Lancashire. He could not face the nostalgic ordeal and, instead, wrote 'At Lord's', the manuscript of which was not found until after his death. After the eventful Gloucester match two stands were erected with all speed for the visit of the Australians on their first English tour. They were filled in spite of bad weather and a not very exciting game was enlivened by Australian Charles Bannerman's hitting, and a spectacular throw in by the Rev. Vernon Royle, one of the most brilliant of all cover points—to judge from the records almost if not quite up to the Washbrook and Hobbs standards—to run out Arthur Bannerman. This was the first time in history that an Australian team (apart from the 'Abos'), played at Old Trafford so that this was, for the young county club, a significant year. Significant rather than conspicuously successful. Lancashire played 10 matches, won 5, drew 2 and lost 3. But, in addition to the events just recorded, Steel revealed his greatness, especially in the Yorkshire match, in which he took 5 wickets for 49 followed by 9 for 63. In this game Hornby and Barlow opened with 87, Barlow's share being 9—but he went on to score sixty.

Barlow's improvement as a bowler was manifest in the return Roses match, which was drawn in spite of his 8 wickets for 22 runs. That season 25-years-old Jack Crossland, who was to be the centrepiece (and victim) of the first really heated throwing rumpus, bowled his first overs for the county, and very fast they were. And O. P. Lancashire, whose apt name was to be linked with the county for many years to come as player and later as President, also made his debut. That first Australian tour was to have a marked influence on English cricket, setting a new standard not only in generally smart appearance on the field but in variations of bowling and keenness in the field. Royle was one of the few fielders in the country who was outstanding even in comparison with the best of the visitors. He had first appeared for Lancashire in 1873, the year in which county cricket was reformed to regularise the qualifications of players, and the county championship began to take shape.

Lancashire had felt itself in a fairly strong position by now with seemingly assured security of tenure at Old Trafford and a team of present strength and future promise. So much so that the club refused to join a proposed championship competition sponsored by Lord's on the grounds that it might encourage gambling and that, anyway, county cricket was becoming steadily more popular. Four matches were won during that—Lancashire's tenth—season and three lost, two of them to Yorkshire.

The Roses match at Old Trafford was brief but not without interest. Only 212 overs were bowled and 259 runs scored. For Lancashire Appleby had 50 overs, of which 36 were maidens, and for Yorkshire, Alan Hill, from that formidable nursery, Kirkheaton (Hirst and Rhodes were born there too) bowled 24 maidens in his 53 overs, taking 8 match wickets for 47 runs. Tom Emmett had set Lancashire on the path to destruction with a first innings analysis of 7 for 29. Between the Roses defeats, however, Lancashire decisively beat Surrey (by an innings and 113) due to Hornby's first championship century, 128, and the only one for the county that season, and the bowling of McIntyre and Watson, who put out the visiting Londoners for 44 and 105. The pair took 107 wickets between them that season. Third in the list was Appleby, with 5.

The following season started dismally with a heavy defeat at Old Trafford by Derbyshire, who dismissed Lancashire for 38. The two Roses matches were each lost by the home side. At Old Trafford all forty wickets produced only 318 runs. Rowley won the toss and put Yorkshire in, which seemed an astute enough decision when they were all out for 96. But Lancashire could only reverse these figures. Hill and Emmett bowled unchanged through the match, taking 10 wickets for 38 and 8 for 74 respectively. In the return game McIntyre's figures were startling—13 wickets for 66 runs in 75·3 overs of which 44 were maidens.

Lancashire in 1875 won 4 out of 6 games and lost only one, to Yorkshire. However both matches with their deadly rivals were hard fought, the first one, at Old Trafford, being of rather more than passing interest. Yorkshire recovered after a disappointing first innings effort which left them 71 runs behind, and the total of 148 wanted by Lancashire to win looked formidable. But Hornby and Bralow, the latter unusually brisk, knocked off the runs, achieving in this laudable process Lancashire's first century opening partnership. For once Barlow headed Hornby in the batting averages, but only just.

Five won and five lost was the tally the next season, which could be called in Lancashire annals 'McIntyre's year'. In those ten games, remarkable for the absence of a single draw, he took 89 wickets costing 11 runs each. Hill, who obviously relished Old Trafford, disposed of 6 Lancashire batsmen, 5 of them clean bowled, for 24 runs; and Yorkshire's George ('Happy Jack') Ulyett took 4 for 14, an ominous warning of what was to become a menace for years to come. Lancashire reversed the results in 1877, winning both Roses matches, the first easily, by 9 wickets, Appleby, backed up by Watson, taking 6 economic wickets and scoring 69 not out. The second game, at Old Trafford, was narrowly won, by 35 runs. The now generally respected openers, Hornby and Barlow hit 92 for the first wicket, Barlow's share being just a quarter of that total. But the hero of the game was a Liverpudlian with a Cambridge blue, W. S. Patterson, whose slow bowling reaped him a harvest of 10 wickets for 130 runs. He improved on this performance against Nottinghamshire, taking 14 wickets as well as hitting a modest top score of 24 in Lancashire's second innings. He finished the season with the remarkable record of 24 wickets costing under ten runs each—from two matches. In fact he played in five more games for the county but did not take another wicket.

In the last year of the formative seventies, Lancashire really looked to have championship potential and, in fact, finished the season at the top of the table jointly with Notts, both counties having lost only one match. A. G. Steel was now recognised as one of the great all-rounders, materially helping Lancashire to an innings win over Yorkshire at Old Trafford by taking 7 of their wickets for 34 runs. His brother, D. Q. Steel, scored a half century. This victory was won during a spell which nearly secured the championship outright. In successive matches Derbyshire were beaten twice, Kent, Yorkshire and Gloucestershire once each. An odd feature of the Kent game at Old Trafford was that Hornby was dropped 7 times during an innings of 61—two more and the sobriquet would presumably have become 'Cat' instead of 'Monkey'.

But Yorkshire ultimately robbed Lancashire of the title upon which they had set their eyes and hearts. It was a convincing victory, to say the least of it, by an innings and 60 runs. The chief destroyers were Ulyett and Bates, who hit the first century of all in the Roses encounters. Two young Lancashire recruits showed some promise, G. Nash, who took 5 Notts wickets and J. (for Johnny) Briggs, who failed to reveal the bowling form which was to bring him so many wickets for Lancashire and for England, but signalled his arrival in first class cricket with 36 useful runs. Lancashire were on the threshold of a golden era, the longed for title champion county soon to be their's for the first, but most certainly not the last time.

3 *Triumph and Trouble*

The 1880s were, for Lancashire, years of triumph—and trouble. The county's success, the peak their championship in 1881 without the loss of a single game, was marred by controversy over the actions of some of their bowlers and the club's habit of recruiting players from outside the county's boundaries. There had been a good deal of criticism of this 'open house' policy, with special reference to the fact that, in the year of their first county championship, Barlow was the only professional in the side who was actually Lancashire born. Surrey were to face similar strictures for imitating the Lancashire practice.

But in 1880, at least, the northerners could point with pride to the fact that their new captain and leading batsman, Hornby, like their star professional all-rounder, Barlow, was one hundred per cent Lancastrian. From the bowling angle it was a season of transition. William McIntyre, from Nottingham, who, for ten years, had been one of the most accurate fast bowlers in the country—according to the records he never bowled a wide—inexplicably faded away and had to be dropped. He had taken 456 wickets for the county, averaging below 11 runs each. Though Nash and Watson—the latter took 79 wickets, his highest aggregate—ably assisted by Barlow and Appleby, helped the side to gain six victories from twelve matches, McIntyre was clearly missed.

Crossland, of the suspect action, was not yet the menace he was to become before the rumpus over his 'chucking' untimely ended his career, but Pilling proved himself as good a wicketkeeper as there was in England. Surrey were beaten twice, at Old Trafford and the Oval, the second Lancashire win rightly securing an honoured place in history. Lancashire were 110 behind on the first innings and defeat loomed. But Hornby, hitting lustily and running between the wickets as if pursued by flames, scored a century—again the only one of the season—dramatically to reverse the situation. Surrey failed by sixty runs to obtain the 202 runs the inspired

Hornby and his men had set them. Two defeats by champions Nottinghamshire were depressing features of that summer.

'Rain stopped play', a not altogether unfamiliar aspect of Old Trafford cricket, was a dismal burden indeed for Yorkshire to suffer in the Roses match. They needed only 51 runs with all wickets standing, after Peate had hustled out Lancashire for 47, taking 8 wickets for 24, when the rains came. Barlow, who had scored 3 in the first innings while Hornby hit 42, had the distinction, familiar to him, of carrying his bat through the entire innings— scoring 10.

A seemingly trivial event which was to have marked significance for Lancashire and, more particularly, for Old Trafford, took place before the start of that frustrating (from the visitors' viewpoint) fixture. Spectators were then allowed, before the start of play, to stroll about the ground, except, of course, on the table, which would be gravely surveyed from a respectful distance by those who knew they knew better than the captains whether or not it would be expedient to bat first. Among the 'experts' that morning was a boy named William Howard who, having left school at the age of twelve, was in the habit of walking six miles from his home to Old Trafford early in the morning before the gatemen arrived, and hiding himself somewhere on the ground until play started. He had been caught and gently but firmly ejected so, upon this fine morning, he decided to emerge from his lair and mingle with the crowd, in the hope of seeing his idol, Mr Hornby, as well as avoiding detection. To his delight Mr Hornby came out of the pavilion to contemplate the scene, whereupon young Howard, screwing up every vestige of his courage (and spotting that the great man appeared to be in a good humour) approached him and asked if he could use the ground free and, in return, make himself useful. Mr Hornby, touched by the boy's enthusiasm and sheer cheek, agreed.

William (as he was always called, never Bill), remained at Old Trafford for fifty years and its activities may be said to have revolved round him. So much so that, when he wrote a book at once highly discursive and deeply affectionate called, simply, *Fifty Years' Cricket Reminiscences of a Non-Player* the title page proclaimed the author thus:

W. E. Howard
Old Trafford.

Sir Neville Cardus, in a preface, wrote: 'His duties in the pavilion have always been manifold and endless; the general aim of them is to make Old Trafford as comfortable a cricket ground as any in England.' William Howard was appointed, in 1888, to take charge of the pavilion and amateur dressings rooms and this was, roughly, his position more than half a century later. But he was much more —*major domo*, adviser to young pros, confidant of old amateurs, philosopher and friend to all true Old Trafford believers. When William's unique career started, the old pavilion (pulled down in 1894 to make way for the present building) was picturesque but small. There was one spacious dressing room for the amateurs. The professionals changed on the 'popular' side of the ground, in a room somewhat cramped and lacking in any sort of amenities. For county matches a tent was put up to accommodate lady sub-scribers, few in number but boundless in enthusiasm. It is reported that two of them arrived at 7 a.m. for an important game—and were still there in the evening though the rain had been such that there never was a chance of any play.

Old Trafford was in the country then. The ground was reached by a narrow footpath across the meadows from Old Trafford station. Those who arrived by road used carriages, buggies, farm-carts, horses, ponies or just their own feet—according to financial status—to enter the ground via Warwick Road and Chester Road. On one occasion during a club match a covey of partridges landed on the playing area, having been flushed by a farmer cutting hay in an adjoining field. Mr S. H. Swire, who had played for Lanca-shire in the clubs earliest games and did much for the new county club, managed to bag a couple. Professionals were still basically paid bowlers and were liable to be reminded of that status. Protests against amateur demands on their services were rare but William recalled one which caused much amusement, except to the gentle-man concerned. Members were permitted to practise between 2 p.m. and 7 p.m. One evening, when the light was poor and it was past 6 o'clock the pros decided it would be safe to change and go home. As they were about to depart a member emerged from the pavilion and demanded two bowlers. With haste and many a curse two of the pros changed back, then proceeded to the nets—bearing lighted candles, which they ceremonially placed beside the stumps.

The next season, 1881, was one of the greatest in the Lancashire story. Ten matches were won outright, six by an innings, three were drawn, in Lancashire's favour, and none lost. Lancashire finished that unforgettable summer runaway champions, so much so that *Wisden* recorded: 'A series of brilliant successes almost un-paralleled in the history of county cricket.' The word 'almost' was, surely, superfluous. The Lancashire team was, without doubt, one of the most powerful in the history of the club and the most powerful up to that year. At full strength this was the batting order, which promised runs all the way down, certainly to number 9: Hornby, Barlow, Steel, Robinson, Briggs, Watson, Royle, Lancashire, Crossland, Nash, Pilling.

How it would have compared with the great sides of Johnny Tyldesley's era before the first world war, or the epoch of Ernest Tyldesley and the all-conquering sides of the late twenties, can only be a matter for grandstand, or fireside conjecture, but, with all that batting strength, five bowlers of real class and one of the best wicket-keepers in all cricket, this was a formidable combination indeed. Hornby was the outstanding batsman in England, despite the far from negligible efforts of W. G. Grace and W. W. Read. He hit three centuries, the most glorious of them 188 against Derbyshire, the highest score of his career, to the untrammelled delight of a con-siderable Old Trafford crowd. The bowlers having disposed of Derby for 102, my Hornby and my Barlow achieved their highest opening partnership to date, 157. It was characteristic. When Barlow was out for 35 Hornby's score was 118. Against Kent he had another century and was ably assisted by W. Robinson— another Yorkshireman to give years of faithful service to the rival club—who scored 90. Lancashire pride was high and Lancastrian chests fully expanded when Yorkshire were beaten for the second time that season. The first Roses game, at Sheffield, had been one of the most exciting of all. Neither side had been beaten. The heroes of a heroic struggle were Barlow, who scored 69, and bowlers Nash and H. Miller, an amateur who appeared in only five matches for the county in the course of which he took 10 wickets.

At Old Trafford A. G. Steel was Yorkshire's scourge, taking 7 wickets for 59 runs in the first innings, 13 in the match, and scoring fifty including the winning hit. Ironically, he was the destroyer of Lancashire in the one reverse of that historic season. Playing for Cambridge University against his own county in a gala match to mark the opening of Liverpool's new ground at Aigburgh, Steel, with his accurate leg-breaks, took 11 wickets for 91, including 6 for 22 in Lancashire's first innings. Cambridge had a very strong side. The first three batsmen were Studds: G. B. (who carried his bat, scoring 106 out of a total of 187), J. E. K., and C. T.

Lower down the order there were three Lancashire players, Steel, O. P. Lancashire and J. R. Napier. Steel again bowled splendidly in the benefit match at Old Trafford for McIntyre, who had retired after his decline the year before. Inevitably (in those days) the Gloucestershire match was chosen, and Steel had the distinction of bowling W. G. twice. He and Watson contemptuously dismissed Gloucester for 42—on a batsmen's wicket. But the most remarkable match of an eventful year was played at the Oval. Lancashire were all out for 78 in less than 90 minutes, a Surrey amateur, J. J. Parfitt, taking 7 wickets for 33 runs. Surrey then contrived to get well inside this record, their innings ending in less than one hour, at 36. Crossland decisively beat Parfitt's record with 7 for 14. He and Watson demolished Surrey between them; Hornby, Barlow and Robinson made the necessary runs.

Crossland was now, whatever his action, very, very fast. It was recorded that, when he was playing for the county against 22 colts at Nantwich, he hit a young batsman on the knuckles, then the knee. The batsman started to walk to the pavilion but the umpire called him back. 'You're not out,' he said. 'I know that,' the batsman replied, 'but I'm going.' Not only colts but experienced county players quailed at the Crossland expresses in 1882, when Lancashire stayed at the top of the championship table but had to share the honours with Nottinghamshire.

Crossland was now acknowledged to be the fastest bowler in England, and certainly he was the most controversial. He was assailed mainly for throwing but the fact that he had no qualification to play for Lancashire brought him under fire too. During the winter of 1881–2 James Lillywhite had written, in *Lillywhite's Companion*, a reasoned protest against his bowling action. The Australians also made their objections known after a match in which they only narrowly beat the county side. Crossland, that season during which the 'chucking' row simmered, took 93 wickets costing 10· runs each, but the outstanding player was Barlow. He headed both batting and bowling averages, a feat unparalleled in Lancashire's history; and never was he more dogged. Three times he carried his bat right through the innings. Against Notts he scored 8 in 1 hour 20 minutes, and 5 in $2\frac{1}{2}$ hours; and in the return match he had 44 in 2¼ hours and 49 in 5¼ hours—an aggregate of 106 runs in 11 hours 20 minutes. Lancashire lost their chance of an outright championship in that first Notts game.

Towards the end of the season notable for, among other events, a fall of snow at Old Trafford in June; the Crossland rumpus began to boil. At the Oval there were hostile demonstrations when Crossland was put on, and again when Lancashire left the field after he had bowled with such ferocity that he had taken 5 wickets for 1 run in his first spell; he had 11 for 79 in the match. Back at Old Trafford Lancashire beat Middlesex, which brought the climax nearer. Middlesex refused to renew the fixture on the ground that Crossland's action was unfair, and Notts followed suit at the end of the season. This provoked a wrathful reply from the Lancashire President, former captain E. B. Rowley. At the annual meeting he thundered: 'It is most superfluous on the part of Notts to object to the Lancashire bowler and to take upon themselves the work of the umpires.' He suggested that the M.C.C. were quite capable of dealing with the matter and, if they were not, they should be 'done away with' and replaced by a body of cricketers.

There had been, that season, an even more ugly demonstration at the Oval, threatening to enforce abandonment of the match. This time the row spread into the pavilion. It became so acrimonious after the Surrey innings that play had to be held up for half an hour. That winter there were more bitter exchanges between Lancashire and Nottinghamshire. After the former had sent a provocative Christmas card to Trent Bridge, the latter replied with a New Year's 'greeting' card. It read: 'Lancashire County Cricket. The only rules necessary for players in the county XI are that they shall neither have been born in, nor reside in, Lancashire. Sutton-in-Ashfield men will have the preference.'

Not only Crossland, but Nash and Watson, though they were slow bowlers, were the subject of controversy. In 1884 Notts broke off fixtures with this terse statement: 'Nottinghamshire declines to play Lancashire this season for the following reason, that Lancashire have, during the last season, played in their eleven at least two men as to the fairness of whose bowling there is grave doubt.' And Lord Harris, the Kent captain, joined in the row, objecting to the selection of Crossland to play for England against the Australians at Old Trafford (at that time the selection was left to the authorities on the ground where the match was to be played).

Lancashire retorted that they intended to include their own fast bowler and added: 'We suppose under the circumstances the English team will lose your valuable assistance, which we regret very much.' Crossland, in fact, was left out and never did play in a Test match (the Test was drawn, the records laconically noting that 'rain spoiled play'). The long drawn out affair came to a head the following year. Lancashire beat Kent at Old Trafford and Lord Harris promptly wrote a long letter alleging that both Nash and Crossland threw, and announcing that he intended to ask Kent to allow the return fixture to go by default. Lancashire replied that Nash and Crossland had appeared at Lord's and had never been no-balled there for throwing and that Crossland had been selected by M.C.C. the previous season to play for the North. The correspondence was forwarded to M.C.C. At last the sour and protracted squabble ended, and in an odd manner. M.C.C. disqualified Crossland—for having broken his residential qualification by living in Nottingham for some months. He played his last match against Cheshire in June.

Those three years of strife had seen some decline in Lancashire's supremacy. In 1883 they seemed set for another championship but fell apart in the second half of the programme. The season's outstanding feat was a spectacular victory, by 70 runs, over Kent at Old Trafford after following on 103 runs behind. Hornby scored 96, after 88 in the first innings, and Kent collapsed on a worn wicket. It was at Old Trafford that Yorkshire ended Lancashire hopes of another championship, beating them by 8 wickets. A Yorkshire cobbler, A. G. Harrison, known as 'Shoey', started the rot with fast bowling which gained him 7 wickets for 43 in Lancashire's first innings; in the return he had eight wickets, 5 for 21 in Lancashire's first innings. Yorkshire won again at Old Trafford the following year, but this was a game to remember, very much alive to the last over. Ulyett was the decisive factor, taking 5 Lancashire wickets for 38 runs and then, almost alone, resisting the wiles of Watson to hit 32 out of the 97 Yorkshire managed to reach after losing 7 wickets.

4 *Incomparable Johnny*

To offset the dismal Crossland affair, Johnny Briggs emerged during the season of 1885 as a slow left-arm bowler of great potential, as well as a more than valuable bat. In fact, that summer he took 79 wickets costing only 10 runs each, compared with 18 at 22 runs apiece the year before. He was also concerned in a batting feat which stood as a world record until 1899 and is still a Lancashire record. He and Pilling put on 173 for the last wicket against Surrey, Briggs going on to compile 186, his highest score in first class cricket. Pilling's 61 not out was his highest, too. Briggs, small, warm, youthful, as Lancashire as Old Trafford itself though he was, in fact, born in Notts—the family moved to Lancashire when he was a small boy—was, at first, primarily a batsman. But the opportunity revealed him as a great bowler, and 11 wickets against Australia at Lord's underlined the fact. He owed his start in big cricket to Barlow, who saw him playing in a benefit match at Liverpool when he was only 14. He recommended the boy to S. H. Swire (by now the Lancashire C.C.C.'s Monorary Secretary (he remained in that post until the 'Hon' disappeared) who put him on the ground staff. He then moved into Barlow's home and the pair subsequently played together not only for Lancashire but for England. Indeed, after a Lord's Test a London newspaper burst into a gushing paeon, the last lines of which read:

> 'Here's your health, ye glorious three!
> 'Barlow, Briggs and Shrewsbury.'

The limelight moved briefly from Barlow and Briggs to an amateur, G. M. Kemp, later Lord Rochdale, during 1885. He had the distinction of scoring the first century (109) for Lancashire against Yorkshire. It proved to be his only hundred, his highest score and almost a third of his aggregate of runs for the county—335 runs in 18 matches—but he certainly relished the Yorkshire bowling; in the following season he took two centuries off their usually formidable bowlers, 125 and 103, both for Cambridge University. Subsequently politics claimed him, first in the Commons, then the Lords, but a deep interest in Lancashire cricket remained with him until his death, in 1945, in his 80th year.

Briggs, in first class cricket scored 13,983 runs and took 2,201 wickets, 97 of them against Australia. In South Africa he set up a record unique—15 wickets (14 of them bowled) for 28 runs for England at Cape Town. And he remains the only player to have hit a century and performed the hat trick against Australia. He remains, too, the only one who has taken 1,000 wickets and scored more than 10,000 runs for Lancashire. Three times he hit a century and took 10 or more match wickets.

He was a merry soul, full of irrepressible humour and adored by the Old Trafford regulars. But his end was tragic. He had a mental breakdown, appeared to recover, and, indeed, added to his fabulous record of achievements 'all ten' (for 55 runs) against Warwickshire in 1900, but relapsed and died in 1902 at the age of 39.

Barlow's benefit match in 1886 was felicitous in every sense. The rift with Notts and Kent had been healed and the former, champions for four seasons, were choosen for the occasion. The 11,000 spectators at Old Trafford upon the first day watched, entranced, what they had dreamed of, a Barlow-Hornby century partnership. The total attendance exceeded 27,000 and the benefit fund £1,000, a highly gratifying sum then. The Kent game, played in June, apart from the happy reunion aspect, was memorable for thick fog which prevented play on the first day. When it cleared an amateur, A. Teggin, took 10 wickets in the match for 87 runs. He played in 5 other matches that season, taking only a further 6 wickets, and vanished from the scene. So did Bennett Hudson, a Yorkshireman who had played for a number of clubs in and out of that county, whose debut for Lancashire was spectacular, a whirlwind 98, including 15 fours, off the Sussex bowling. He was included in the side as a bowler, but his 5 county matches brought him only 3 wickets. However, he took into exile what must certainly be the quickest earned cap—thrown at him out of the pavilion window at the end of his first innings on his first day in first class cricket.

Barlow's bowling and Steel's batting were decisive factors in a four wickets victory over Yorkshire at Old Trafford. Barlow took

6 wickets in each innings. Steel scored 55 out of a puny 112 and a superb 80 not out towards the 178 Lancashire needed to win. But for Lancashire it was not a season of real lustre. Only 5 of the 14 matches were won, 5 lost and 4 drawn. The county had, however, the rare distinction of supplying four players in the England team against Australia at Old Trafford—Barlow, Briggs, A. G. Steel and Pilling—and there would have been five had not Hornby been 'maimed' to use the gruesome current description. It proved to be Barlow's match. He took 8 wickets, held 3 catches and was only once out in scoring 68 runs. F. R. Spofforth, the 'demon bowler', with the most menacing bound and flailing arms at the end of his charging run-up, was also 'maimed' but, in another game at Old Trafford, against the North of England, he achieved one of his more impressive feats, 7 wickets for 19 runs.

The year of Queen Victoria's Jubilee, with all its pomp and pageantry, was one of considerable achievement and, perhaps, even greater portent, for Lancashire C.C.C. It is true that Yorkshire, in loyal jubilee mood, put up the record 'Roses' score, 590 which included an aggressive 160 by Louis Hall, another century by Fred Lee, and a robust half century by Lord Hawke, but Lancashire's reply was spirited.

Hornby saved his side with a masterly 92 which ensured another Roses record, 1,220 runs for the loss of 28 wickets. Lancashire's bid for the championship proved abortive only in the last game. Ten out of fourteen matches were won and two players whose names were to shine in the county's story, Frank Sugg and Arthur Mold, drew attention to their potential. Twenty-five years old Sugg, having played cricket for both Yorkshire and Derbyshire (where he was born), and soccer for Burnley and Derby County, was welcomed with much thankfulness to a team sadly lacking batting solidarity. He hit 403 runs in 7 games, a remarkable start to a remarkable career, or third career. Mold, from Northampton, was encountered only in a 'friendly', but he looked, to say the least of it, a likely fast bowler, which he proved to be when Lancashire secured his services in 1889. The return Roses match at Old Trafford was followed with more close attention than any in England that grand summer. Yorkshire once more piled up the runs, 414 of them, at which score Lord Hawke had 125 to his credit from creditably free batting. Then the Yorkshire bowlers, and in particular Peel (who had hit 66) and Emmett, diddled

Lancashire to defeat and the loss of the championship to Surrey. There was, to be sure, some justice in this. Surrey, at Old Trafford, had also handsomely beaten their eventual runners-up, Walter Read dominating the Lancashire bowling to amass 247.

One incident, a near tragedy, marred a happy season at Old Trafford. When Gloucestershire were in the field A. C. M. Croome, trying to make a running catch, fell on the spiked railings and was so badly hurt that, for some time, he was not expected to live. Lancashire sagged a little in 1888, falling to fifth place, but it was an eventful enough season which included a remarkable occasion known for ever as 'Napier's match'. The Rev. John Russell Napier, who had played with A. G. Steel in the Marlborough XI and missed a Cambridge blue only through injury, was a surprise choice for Lancashire's fixture with the Australians. He was a big, cheerful character more popular with his flock at Preston than with opposing batsmen. For he was fast and, though not un-Christian enough to bowl deliberate bumpers, certainly bowled balls which kicked disconcertingly. Lancashire batted first and were out for 98, which was not expected by anyone present to be a winning score. The Australians, however, found the combination of Napier and Briggs formidable and could only retaliate with 163. Lancashire, in their second innings, hit 154 and collection by the Australians of a mere 90 runs to win looked like a formality. The first wicket fell, to Napier, at 11. When Jones, the victim, returned to the pavilion he issued this grim warning: 'Look after your heads, boys, when you go in to bat, that chap's dangerous.'

Whether or not these doleful tidings caused demoralisation, it is irrefutably upon record that all the Australians were out with the scoreboard showing 66 runs, leaving the county totally unexpected victors by 23 runs. Napier took 4 wickets for 48 (having been Lancashire top second innings scorer with 37), Briggs 5 for 15. His schoolboy friend Steel was so overjoyed that he suggested that the score should be printed on silk as a memento, a course adopted with enthusiasm. Napier only played for Lancashire once more, again with sensational success. This was in a Roses match the same summer, at Sheffield. Yorkshire had passed the poor Lancashire total, 54, painfully achieved on a soft pitch, for the loss of only one wicket. Hornby had not used Napier but, after advice from the crowd: 'Put the parson on' he did so. Yorkshire were then 80 for 5. Napier finished the innings at that total, taking 4 wickets for no runs in 3 maiden overs. His two match first class career ended with a batting average of 24 and a bowling average of 9·27 (for 11 wickets). But the season belonged to Briggs. Derbyshire were put out for 17, the lowest score by an opposing county in Lancashire's history, and Briggs had a match record of 13 wickets for 39 runs. Twice more he took 13 wickets—against Middlesex and the Australians, and once he took twelve, v Gloucester. He headed the first class bowling averages with 187 wickets costing a shade over 9 runs each, and he had the distinction of appearing in the first of those 'cricketers of the year' features in *Wisden*, entitled 'Six great bowlers of the year'.

He came first in the list followed by the devastating Australian pair, C. T. B. Turner and J. J. Ferris, with their truly astonishing hauls of 314 and 220 wickets respectively, George Lohmann, of Surrey (253), Bobby Peel of Yorkshire (181), and S. M. J. ('Sammy') Woods of Somerset. Rivals Briggs and Peel had a rare struggle for supremacy in the eternal battle at Old Trafford. Peel took 5 for 32 in Lancashire's first innings total of 79 and, to the utter dismay of all devout Tykes, Yorkshire fell short of this modest aggregate by 28 runs, Briggs taking 6 of their wickets for 24 runs. Peel's reply was 7 for 30 in Lancashire's second innings and as tense a match as any in the series-without-end (we hope) resulted in a Yorkshire win by two wickets.

Briggs in the following year, significant not only for ending at the threshold of the gay nineties but for the fact that the 4-ball over was changed to the 5-ball over, was second in the first class bowling average (only fractionally below Attewell of Notts) followed by two other Lancashire bowlers, Mold and Watson. Mold had established himself from his first match as a menacingly fast bowler; indeed he was soon to be regarded as the most dangerous in the country. Making his debut that season with Mold was Albert Ward, another migrant from Yorkshire where he had not achieved much success. His first season for Lancashire, however, earned him a place among *Wisden*'s 'Nine great batsmen of the year'. He headed the county's batting averages, hit the most runs and had the highest score, 114 not out, a resounding start to a career which was to bring him more than 15,000 runs in 15 seasons with an average of over 30 and an even higher one in Test matches, 37·46. Yorkshire were beaten twice, Briggs and Mold playing leading roles in these dramas. The Huddersfield match was a thriller, Lancashire winning by 3 runs when Yorkshire, needing only 75, had looked certain of victory. Briggs kept an immaculate length while Mold bowled with such fire that he took 13 wickets for 111 runs. And the bold hitting of Briggs, especially afer he had been dropped, was another vital factor. In the return fixture Briggs took 10 wickets and Yorkshire won by 10 wickets.

The last season of the '80s drew to its close on a slightly sour note. There had been criticism about the lack of stamina in the Old Trafford pitch. So an outside expert, from Nottingham, was called in to advise Reynolds and remedial measures were taken that winter. Apparently they were successful for the grousing stopped. And certainly in the nineties both batsmen and bowlers had cause to think kindly of the Old Trafford wicket. Surrey, in 1890, demonstrated their right to the championship, beating Lancashire, the runners-up, in both fixtures. The bowlers of both teams dominated the Old Trafford match. It was, in fact, all over in seven hours, Lohmann emerging as the most successful player with 13 wickets for 54 runs. Johnny Briggs, though out of the game for a month through injury, had a wonderful season. He took 86 wickets for Lancashire and 158 altogether.

Against Yorkshire he hit two half centuries; Mold, bowling at great speed, took 8 wickets for 38 runs and only rain saved the visitors. Against Sussex, Briggs scored 129 not out at a run a minute and took 10 wickets for 41 runs in the match—truly a giant's share. Watson's analyses were, to be sure, even more startling, 5 for 7 and 4 for 6. To the sorrow of all Lancashire, Pilling, who had been seriously ill, was unable to play at all. The club had sent him to Australia in the hope that he would recover but he continued to decline and died the following year. Impartial critics gave him the edge over George Pinder of Yorkshire, certainly his nearest rival behind the stumps. Considering how few matches were played during his 12 years of service, from 1877 to 1889, compared with more recent times, his record was quite remarkable. To this day he is listed second only to George Duckworth, who played in 424 matches for the county from 1923 to 1938—and 24 times for England. In 173 games for Lancashire, Pilling's victims numbered 465—149 stumped and 316 caught, constituting more 'scalps' per game than any other Lancashire wicketkeeper. Moreover, his example had been invaluable, and, with his departure from the game the standard of fielding fell sadly.

There was, however, a bright side to the Lancashire picture. Nineteen-years-old, Manchester-born, Archibald Campbell Mac-Laren played his first game for the county. He had an impressive record at Harrow School immediately behind him. His feats there included 55 and 67 against Eton at the age of fifteen, and that year, his last, 76 out of 133. What a debut that was! The match was against Sussex at Hove. Albert Ward, Barlow and Sugg were all out with 23 runs between them when MacLaren went to the wicket. In just 130 minutes he hit 108 runs and the soundness of his technique, the flow of his strokes and his intelligent anticipation left no doubt at all that a new county and Test star had arisen.

5 Near-Miss Nineties

During 1891 young MacLaren played in only five county matches and failed to record another century. But he headed the batting averages, followed by Albert Ward, and the pair put on 215 for the 3rd wicket against Kent, which assured his first entry under the heading 'Productive Partnerships' in a booklet *Lancashire County Cricket Records* by T. Swindells, published in 1908. Ward and MacLaren made a number of further appearances therein but the most productive partnership in which MacLaren figured was with A. Paul, the couple together scoring 363 against Somerset in 1895. MacLaren was also listed with Sugg, Briggs, J. T. Tyldesley (how very productive were their joint efforts) H. G. Garnett, J. Hallows, E. E. Steel, F. H. Hollins, R. H. Spooner, A. H. Hornby and (returning to the early nineties) Albert Smith, of Oldham, a newly-joined professional with whom he put on 208 for the 3rd wicket against Sussex in 1892.

The saddest aspect of season 1891 had been the end of the immortal Hornby-Barlow association. Barlow's form, it was clear to all who saw him play, if not to himself, had diminished. His last first class match for Lancashire, like his first twenty years earlier, was against Yorkshire. He scored nine and did not bowl. Barlow was convinced that he should have been allowed to play on. In a book he wrote: 'I always considered, like a great many more, that I was left out of the county team far too soon. As W.G. remarks in his book on Cricket: "Barlow was left out of the Lancashire team long before he had lost his form" '. Certainly he had taken the Old Man's wicket on a number of occasions, earning the profound respect of that formidable character.

Unlike Barlow, Mold had a splendid season. In the two Somerset matches he took a total of 26 wickets for 240 runs which made this, their first season in the county championship, memorable for the west countrymen. He also took 20 wickets in both the Gloucester and the Sussex games and headed the averages with 129 wickets costing only 12·62 runs each. He was ably supported by Johnny Briggs, who wrought the destruction of Yorkshire (for the second time that summer) taking 8 wickets for 46 runs after Yorkshire had followed on. Lancashire were runners-up to Surrey. As in '91 so in '92, Lancashire started badly, then pulled themselves together but not sufficiently sternly to challenge for the championship. It was, indeed, a decade of near-misses. Captaincy difficulties were one factor. For two years A. N. Hornby and S. M. Crossfield shared the position, never a very satisfactory solution, then A. C. MacLaren took over for three years, handed back to Hornby and, in the last season of the century, shared the captaincy with G. R. Bardswell. Hornby, in fact, played only three times in the seasons 1892 and 1893 and MacLaren could not play regularly in '96 or '97. Lancashire did win the title once, in 1897, were second three times, fourth three times and sixth once.

The 1892 season opened with an encouraging win over Sussex. The game was remarkable for the bowling of Humphreys, who took 8 Lancashire second innings wickets—with lobs. If it did have its disappointments for Lancashire, the season could not be called uneventful. Yorkshire won the first of the Roses games by 4 wickets amid much tension but were thoroughly trounced for this piece of impudence in the return match at Old Trafford. Ward hit 180 and Briggs 115 before the Yorkshire bowlers transformed a Lancashire score of 437 for 4 into 471 all out. Yorkshire were out for 209, Briggs bowling unchanged to take 8 wickets for 113 runs in 50 overs. Making the ball lift nastily Briggs and Watson pulverised Yorkshire in the second innings to gain a red rose victory by an innings and 83. Even for an all-rounder as good as Johnny Briggs this was a remarkable achievement. Spectacular, too, was Lancashire's win over Somerset at Old Trafford—in one day. Somerset scored 88 and 58, Briggs taking 12 wickets for 83 runs, Mold 8 for 40. Play was extended to allow Lancashire to knock off the few runs needed, which was a sporting gesture on the part of Somerset, whose bowlers had dismissed them for 116. Mold virtually annihilated Kent, the ball flying menacingly after rain to give him 9 for 29 in Kent's second innings and 13 for 91 in the match. He also achieved the remarkable feat, for so fast a bowler, of taking 14 Sussex wickets for 159 runs in the course of 53·3 (five-ball) overs all in one day.

Lancashire surrendered a fair chance to win the championship in

1893 when they lost the last two matches to Nottinghamshire and Middlesex, allowing Yorkshire, victorious in their last three fixtures, to head them. To offset, to some extent, this dolorous comparison, Lancashire had the satisfaction of beating their rivals in both Roses matches. At Headingley the ferocity of Mold and the subtlety of Briggs made the Yorkshire batting look frailer than it had been and was to be. Briggs, in the second innings, had the astonishing figures, against the coming champions, of 8 wickets for 19 runs. The Old Trafford game, with the drama of another Peel v. Briggs duel within the greater drama of the most dramatic match in the Roses series, ended in a scarcely credible victory for Lancashire, by six runs. It has been described as the 'mad' Roses match, hailed as the greatest of all and firmly assessed, by William Howard, as the most sensational match he ever witnessed, 'full of thrills from the start to the finish'. Lancashire's totals, 64 and 50, hardly seemed to point towards triumph even though Yorkshire had managed only 58 in their first innings. And when A. Sellers (father of that fine Yorkshire captain, in later years Brian Sellers), and that great all-rounder F. S. Jackson, opening for Yorkshire, had put on 24 of the 57 runs needed, Lancashire's defeat looked certain.

Indeed Briggs, after his first spell of bowling, said to Sellers: 'I think it's all over now, sir, bar shouting.' Shortly after this procrastination William Oakley, a bowler who had a brief career with Lancashire and had replaced Briggs, rapped Jackson upon the pads and appealed. The umpire rejected the appeal. The next ball also hit Jackson's pad and, as it ran away towards square leg he started to run. Again the bowler appealed, and up went the umpire's hand. Sellers, observing this, stayed where he was, calling to Jackson: 'He has given you out.' Jacker replied 'Surely not' but took the precaution of trying to scramble back to his crease. Before he could make his ground, however, the ball had been thrown in and A. T. Kemble, the Lancashire wicket-keeper, having broken the wicket, had roared 'Howzat?'

'What for?' the square-leg umpire enquired. 'Stumped,' replied Kemble. 'Not out,' said the umpire, firmly. 'Then, run out,' Kemble suggested. His persistence was rewarded. 'Out,' said the umpire, this time raising his finger high. And out Jackson had to go, umpire's verdicts being unchallengeable in the best cricketing circles. Yorkshire's immortal pair, Brown and Tunnicliffe soon followed and then there was enacted, to the bewilderment of the

already bemused crowd of 28,000, a further tragi-farce. Ernest
Smith, of Yorkshire, a schoolmaster and elegant addition to the
holiday scene, hit a low drive which looked a certain boundary.
Crossfield dived to earth and threw the ball up in the air. After
some hesitation the umpire again raised his finger.

Smith was clearly dumbfounded and remained at the wicket
until it was borne in upon him that he had been given out. After
that double blow the Yorkshire batting fell to pieces. At 46 for 7
'Happy' Jack Ulyett, who, in his younger days, had opened the
innings for England with W.G., walked nonchalantly to the crease.
He would show 'em, he would. Woodhouse next departed pavilion-
wards and a young chap from Kirkheaton named George Herbert
Hirst appeared at number ten. He attempted a huge pull and was
caught. Hunter the stumper, last man in, hit a single and Ulyett,
facing Briggs, decided that it was now or never in such a desperate
situation. The wily Briggs sent down a ball which not merely demanded, but begged to be hit and Ulyett hit it, hard, high and
surely a certain winning six. It was Yorkshire's match, snatched
from the very jaws of defeat. Or was it? As the cheers broke out
Albert Ward, gazing skywards as he stood with his sturdy back to
the pavilion rails, carefully cupped his large hands. And into the
cup descended the ball. There was pandemonium. The pitch was invaded and the noise was indescribable as pent-up emotions broke
like a tidal wave. Inside the pavilion the din was more subdued, but
full of acrimony. Arguments about the umpiring were fierce. If that
umpire at the bowler's end hadn't given such a sloppy signal that
Sellers had mistaken it for out instead of 'leg bye', Jackson would
have been there yet, or would have won the game; and if the
other umpire hadn't been blind he would have seen that Smith's
drive had hit the ground long before it reached the fielder . . .

And, on the other side they were saying that Mr MacLaren
should never have been given out either. In Lancashire's second
innings an appeal for a catch behind the stumps by Hunter had
been allowed though MacLaren protested that he was 'nowhere
near the ball'. Whether it was 'mad' or not the match was one of the
most extraordinary in first class cricket. Forty wickets fell for 223
runs, the highest individual score was 21 by G. B. Barber of
Lancashire, Peel of Yorkshire took 4 wickets for 15 and 6 for 24,
Briggs for Lancashire 6 for 35 and 5 for 25.

County was liable to come before country in those highly com-

petitive championship days. Albert Ward, who had a fine season
with the bat and came third in the national averages, was selected
for all three Tests against Australia, but stood down from the
Lord's match to play for Lancashire—who responded to this loyal
gesture by making up his pay to the extent of £4. And, of the Old
Trafford Test, *Wisden* complained: 'F. S. Jackson and others who
might have been included were playing for Yorkshire at Brighton.'
This Test match, incidentally, was drawn and was memorable only
for the debut of Tom Richardson, of Surrey, who took 10 wickets
for 156 runs. The Lancashire Committee, showing quite unusual
sensitivity about criticism for importing players from outside the
county, advertised thus: 'Wanted, a few good professional bowlers
for 1894; young men and Lancashire born preferred; a good wicket-
keeper also wanted'.

But, once more in 1894, Lancashire had to depend almost entirely
on Briggs and Mold. They bowled between them 1,586 overs, the
next highest number being 188 delivered by Baker. Mightily as they
strove—Mold took 144 at 11 runs each, Briggs 97 at 15 each, including that of W.G. on four occasions, clean bowled each time—
they were poorly supported by the batsmen. The side's Old
Trafford record was gloomy indeed—six matches lost out of seven
played there in May and June. Johnny Briggs, who deserved a
bumper benefit if any Lancastrian ever did, had the worst of luck.
The game chosen was the Roses fixture at Old Trafford. It started
on an unhappy note. There had been a storm in the night and the
prepared wicket had been covered to ensure that Briggs would not
suffer. But Lord Hawke would not have it. After inspecting the
strip, which was full of runs, under the oilskins which served as
covers, he protested with these words: 'I'm very sorry for Briggs
but I have come here to play county cricket and not for a benefit
match.' A huge Bank Holiday crowd understandably protested too,
with vigour, but the autocratic Yorkshire captain had his way, a
new wicket was cut and the whole game was over in less than two
days. Lancashire's four Test batsmen, Hornby, MacLaren, Ward
and Sugg were all out before a run was scored and the fervent
supporters of Lancashire generally and Briggs in particular had the
unhappy experience of seeing the board read: 'Total, 11; wickets,
7'. Only a spirited rally by bowler Baker and stumper Kemble
enabled the team's total to reach 50.

Yorkshire did not fare much better to start with. They were only

26 runs on with seven men out, one of them, Lord Hawke, bowled by Briggs for a duck—which must have been consolatory for the beneficiary and certainly delighted the far from pro-Hawke spectators—but they pondered on to 152 thanks largely to the dour defiance of wicket-keeper Hunter. On the second day Hirst and Peel crushed Lancashire, Hirst bringing his match record to 10 for 56. Briggs' benefit fund from the curtailed match topped £1,000 which was better than had been hoped for in the game's early stages but less by half that of Peel in the return game, also won by Yorkshire in spite of Johnny's 11 wickets.

Mold had a wonderful season. One of his more spectacular feats was performed at Old Trafford and Somerset were the victims. He took 13 wickets, 11 of them bowled, including the hat trick, for 60 runs. He also had 13 Gloucester wickets, excluding that of W.G., bowled by Briggs twice, for 0 and 5. An event minor but memorable was the appearance of Alfred Shaw for Sussex seven years after his last match for Nottinghamshire. He had qualified by residence and justified himself by performance. He bowled one more over than he had years, 52, and took 4 wickets for 73 runs. Attention was diverted temporarily from Old Trafford by the arrival in the City of Queen Victoria, to be acclaimed with patriotic northern fervour as she opened the £20m. Manchester Ship Canal, an historic event which was to make Manchester the third largest seaport and create much industry in the Trafford Park area.

6 MacLaren The Master

Just as 1905 has always been known as 'Jacker's Year', so 1895 belonged to his distinguished Harrow School contemporary Archie MacLaren. When W.G. achieved the remarkable feat of scoring 1,000 runs in May and then delighted his devotees all over the world with his hundredth hundred it seemed that no star could possibly eclipse him. But MacLaren, who had almost vanished from cricket that season, ensured himself immortality and the right to call that glorious summer his own by way of the most spectacular individual total in the history of first class cricket, 424 scored in 7 hours 50 minutes. This achievement was all the more astonishing because MacLaren had not played at all for five weeks. After a highly successful first tour of Australia on which he finished second in the batting averages after his captain, A. E. Stoddart, with a highest score of 228 to his credit, he had returned later than the rest of the team, missing the start of the programme. He played in two matches, without much success, then took a job as a preparatory school master which kept him out of Lancashire and all cricket for five weeks.

During that time Lancashire lost three matches and the skipper's absence was a source of much criticism among the county's supporters. Back in the side at last against Somerset at Taunton he took Albert Ward in to open with him. The score was 141 when Ward, with 64, departed. It was 504 just 190 minutes later when Paul was out for 177, and it was 792 when MacLaren himself was the seventh victim of the toiling, despairing Somerset bowlers. He had beaten by 80 the previous individual record score, 344 hit by W. G. Grace for the M.C.C. v. Kent and, to this day, no batsman in a county match has come nearer than did Bobby Abel, in 1899, when he scored 357 not out, also against Somerset, at the Oval.

MacLaren, in the majestic style which was supremely his own, hit one six, 62 fours, 11 threes, 37 twos and 63 singles—without a chance until he was well into his third century. No wonder Sammy

Woods, of Brighton College, Cambridge University, Somerset, England and Australia having bowled fast and without avail many a wearying over, recalled the event thus: 'I thought that day would never end. I must have run miles.' MacLaren finished the season, so much of which he had missed, with a century in each of the last three games, on wickets which were far from easy. Yet perhaps the finest innings of them all, in defiance of appalling conditions, was not a century at all but a determined match-winning 52 against the most powerful bowling combination in the country, Lohmann, Richardson, Lockwood, Hayward and Brockwell of Surrey.

MacLaren can scarcely ever have played an innings that was not worth watching. He was much more than a superbly poised technician in the classic mould; there was a fluid grace about every stroke which few batsmen in the game's history have displayed. They flowed from the sweeping back lift to the top of the follow through. So perfect and powerful, indeed, was the pendulum that a backward defensive stroke often penetrated the field. This mastery brought him, for Lancashire, 16,000 runs in 307 matches spread over 24 years, with an average of 33·26 (his bowling was rather less successful—1 wicket, average 254·0!). For England he hit 1,931 runs in 35 Tests, averaging 33·87, and in all first class matches 21,959 runs, average 34. He hit 47 centuries, eight of them at Old Trafford. Apart from his own ground, which he always loved, he must have had a special affection for Sydney. In successive innings during that first tour he scored on that ground 142 and 100, 109 and 50 not out, 61 and 140, and 65. Not even Bradman in the years of his supremacy had a run quite like that. And MacLaren very nearly repeated it when he went to Australia as captain. At Sydney he hit 145 and 73, 116, 167 and 92 successively. There is no parallel in cricket.

As a captain he was inclined to be imperious—and unflappable, to borrow a word applied after his era, to another Mac, Prime Minister Harold Macmillan. He was a field commander rather than a 'base wallah', shrewd and calculating though liable to make decisions which reaped him criticism—certainly when captaining England, which he did in 22 Tests—in the 1902 season.

He had the odd reputation of being an optimist in his private life (and on the race course?), a pessimist in his cricket. At any rate he was dedicated and, possessing a retentive memory and a gift for conversation; for all his life he was able to entertain with a seemingly inexhaustible fund of cricketing stories. MacLaren ended his interrupted 1895 season with a batting average of 58·10 to head Albert Ward, Paul, Sugg and Baker. Mold took 182 wickets (average 13) in championship matches alone, his more notable feats including 16 for 111 v. Kent, 15 for 85 (including four in four balls) against Nottinghamshire and 11 for 128 v. Yorkshire. He also figured in a last wicket stand of 111 against Leicestershire at Old Trafford, with Albert Ward, who carried his bat through the innings. Lancashire, though once more recording a near miss— Surrey had to win the last match of the season to stay ahead of them—had a fine season and were so attractive to watch that 25,000 spectators swarmed into the Old Trafford ground for the Yorkshire game and 20,000 when Kent were the visitors.

Apart from MacLaren's record the most significant event was the arrival of 21 years old John Thomas Tyldesley, who wasted no time about revealing his potential, hitting 152 in his second match, against Warwick and earning from *Wisden* the understatement of the decade: 'The general impression seemed to be that he had a good deal of cricket in him.' Frustration seemed to be Lancashire's lot when they found themselves runners-up again in 1896. The side had been bedevilled not so much by Manchester rain as by unlucky injuries.

Mold played much of the season with an injured hand, yet he took 130 wickets at 17 runs each, rather higher than his previous averages. Briggs was more expensive still, his 122 wickets costing almost 20 runs a piece. Still, the side was formidable enough, with the help of newcomers Hallam and l'Anson, to make all the counties fight, even Yorkshire, who won the championship and were so powerful that six batsmen scored more than 1,000 runs and three bowlers took more than 100 wickets. The Roses match at Old Trafford was tensely exciting, though it very nearly didn't take place. Lancashire wanted to give the Whitsun fixture to the Australian tourists, a departure from tradition which Yorkshire resented. Lancashire then accused Yorkshire of discourtesy in the correspondence but eventually the game was fixed for the beginning of the season. And a splendid battle it proved to be.

In wintry conditions Lancashire struggled, only Frank Sugg, with an heroic 74 out of 87 in 75 minutes, defying the relentless Yorkshire attack. Yorkshire were, not for the first time, baffled by Briggs so that upon the morning of the second day Lancashire started their second innings 27 runs on. They left Yorkshire the task of scoring 167 to win, which looked possible while F. S. Jackson and David Denton were together. But when 'Jacker' was out the game swung first one way then the other. At close of play tension was high indeed. Yorkshire still needed 18 runs to win with only two wickets left. This was accomplished in sunshine the next morning, without loss. Surrey were beaten twice—at Old Trafford by three wickets.

One incident was the subject of much argument in the bars of ground and town. MacLaren had scored two against Gloucestershire when he trod on his wicket. The umpire refused an appeal on the ground that the Lancashire captain had completed his stroke and started to run. He was quite unperturbed by the fairly evident resentment at his survival and scored a polished half century.

The greatest match of all at Old Trafford that season was undoubtedly the England-Australia Test. England had won the first Test at Lord's and the Australians were determined to avenge this reverse. They batted first and piled up 412, to which England replied with a modest 231; it would have been an even less impressive total had not wicket-keeper Dick Lilley, of Notts., defied the ferociously fast Ernest Jones to score 65 invaluable runs. But hero number one in the tremendous struggle was K. S. Ranjitsinhji. While other batsmen strove merely to cling on at one end in England's second innings, none reaching twenty, Ranji, at the other end directed the Australian bowling to all parts of the ground, emerging from the battle undefeated with 154 runs against his illustrious name. Undefeated, but not unscathed; unbowed but bloody.

Once the most daunting spell of really fast, nose-high bowling anyone at Old Trafford had ever beheld nearly proved disastrous. A kicking express from Jones removed the skin from the lobe of Ranji's ear. Afterwards, in reply to a solicitous inquiry from Lilley he nonchalantly dismissed his battle scar.

Said he: 'It was very important to get the head well behind the ball in order to get a good sight of it.' Ranji's fabulous innings, characterised by that precise placing which kept the fields scuttling in bewilderment, left Australia requiring 125 to win. Amid near-frenzied excitement they lost four good wickets for 45 runs and, at 100 for 7, it was anyone's game. Trumble and bowler Kelly prodded purposefully for an hour to get those remaining runs and might not have done so if Lilley had held a catch offered by Kelly. It was his one lapse and, if it did cost the match, it was never held against him as was the catch dropped on the same ground against the same opponents a few years later, to dog poor Fred Tate for the rest of his life. Australia won but it was a great game not only for Ranji but for Tom Richardson, of Surrey. He actually bowled 110 overs in little more than 7 hours—an awesome feat by a fast bowler—taking 13 Australian wickets.

At last, in 1897, while the fanfares were proclaiming the old Queen's Diamond Jubilee, Lancashire ceased to be the perpetual blooming bridesmaid and emerged as the blushing bride. Having been runners-up five times in seven seasons, Lancashire became champions under their old skipper, A. N. Hornby, doubling the job with that of President, though he was aged 50 and had first played for the county 27 years before. Mold and Briggs now had the assistance of Hallam and Willis Cuttell, son of a Yorkshire professional who had, like his father, played for that county. He had moved to Nelson so had a residential qualification. Though he was then 32 his contributions in the next ten years were to be considerable—5,389 runs and 760 wickets. These four bowlers proved to be a formidable band, capturing 420 wickets between them. Cuttell's share was 102. Briggs, however, was the vital factor in the turning of the tide for Lancashire, whose team looked un- likely champions in the first part of the season. In three successive matches he took 36 wickets for 323 runs and Lancashire won 8 of the last 11 games. Deservedly he headed the bowling averages with 155 wickets at 16·51 runs each.

MacLaren once more headed the batting averages (51·70) and hit the highest score, 244, off the Kent bowling, a brilliant innings which included 38 boundaries, mostly from powerful pulls. Frank Sugg was the season's beneficiary and an unlucky one, for play was not possible after the first day of the Kent game at Old Trafford. He and Cuttell played a major part in Lancashire's innings victory over Yorkshire at Old Trafford, a prolonged 9th wicket partnership giving Lancashire a lead of 120. Then the pair remorselessly demolished the old enemy with the ball. Sugg and Cuttell figured in another big stand in the away Roses game the following season, Cuttell saving it by aggregating 125 runs in the match without losing his wicket. This Yorkshire-born all-rounder achieved the distinction of being the first Lancashire player ever to complete the cricketers 'double'. He hit 1,003 runs (average 25·71) and took 114 wickets (average 21·21).

And, heartening for the future in a season during which the champions sank to sixth place in the championship table and saw their Yorkshire rivals take their place, was the rise of J. T. Tyldesley. He headed the county's batting averages with 38·91 and scored 1,918 runs in all first class matches. He put up some startling performances, notably 200 out of a Lancashire total of 464 for 7, in 270 minutes on the opening day of the Derbyshire game, and a stand with MacLaren against Kent which reached 155 runs in just two hours.

The end of the gay (and near-miss) nineties and of the Victorian era was also virtually the end of A. N. Hornby's long and distinguished career as a cricketer. At last he finally relinquished the captaincy. Lancashire once more, inexplicably resorted to duel leadership, MacLaren sharing the post with G. R. Bardsley. Hornby still turned out occasionally. Another amateur, Alec Eccles, sometimes stood in as skipper, this messy lack of consistent leadership having an obvious deleterious effect upon the team's performance and morale. There were misfortunes, too. Briggs, who had replaced Wilfred Rhodes in the England team against the Australians at Leeds (to the wrathful dismay of all Yorkshiremen) broke down after taking 3 wickets for 53 runs on the first day, and was taken to a mental home. It was the sad end of his cricket that year, and he lived to play only one more season. Hallam was also out of the game a good deal of that summer. But there were compensations, particularly in the growing status of Tyldesley and the arrival of two youngsters of promise.

The pair, with markedly contrasting backgrounds, were destined to shine brightly in the Lancashire firmament—Jack Sharp, Everton footballer and Reginald Spooner, a classic batsman who had adorned the Marlborough XI and had hit his first county century for Lancashire II. In his first year in the senior team, against Middlesex he hit 44 in 80 minutes and 83 in 118—off two of the best bowlers in the country, J. T. Hearne and Albert Trott. Another newcomer was a second Hornby, Albert, who played in one match with his distinguished father, A.N., against Leicestershire. In and out was an amateur slow left-arm bowler named J. L. Ainsworth, who took 18 wickets in 3 matches and then vanished from first class cricket. Sidney Webb was another 'import', from

Middlesex, now qualified for Lancashire. He took 30 wickets and was to take nearly 250 more in only five years with the county. But it was Tyldesley's year. He hit 1,868 runs topping the averages with 41·95. Against the Australians at Old Trafford on a difficult wicket he actually scored 56 out of 102 and 42 out of 81. The next highest score in that second innings was 6, by Ward, though the second highest 'scorer' was 'Extras'—16. In the Old Trafford Test Australia saved the game after Jackson and Hayward, of Surrey, had fought back from a desperate situation with such determination that the tourists had to follow on. That Test attracted spectators in numbers without precedent. It was estimated that 10,000 were turned away when the gates were shut on the first two days.

7 *The Golden Age—of Batsmanship*

The new century, its first decade to be known to posterity as 'The Golden Age' of cricket, opened hopefully for Lancashire, finishing the 1900 season runners-up to Yorkshire.

It was, indeed the opening of a new epoch for the county, the epoch of the triumphant trio, MacLaren, Spooner and Tyldesley. The phrase 'Golden Age', firmly established as it is, might have more properly been extended to 'Golden Age of Batsmanship', in which art the men of Lancashire excelled. MacLaren, as fine a bat as England possessed, with Spooner and Tyldesley scarcely less lustrous, was now in sole command. Cricket's following as that shining era dawned, was both great and fervent. And Lancashire's brilliant band of fast scoring stroke makers earned a devout and steadfast following of their own. Not that Lancashire had a monopoly of batting talent, with Ranji and C. B. Fry at Brighton, Warner at Lord's, Hayward and Abel at the Oval, Grace and Jessop at Gloucester. Were the batsmen of the Golden Age, brilliant as they undoubtedly were, pampered a little too much, given almost total priority over the humble, toiling bowlers? There seems to be evidence to support this near-heretical suggestion. Bowlers whose action was in any way suspect were 'called', even banned; pitches not quite pluperfect were severely criticised by the Masters (i.e. the lordly batsmen who were convinced, not unreasonably, that the crowds had come to see them score, not to capitulate to mere bowlers).

The attitude of many followers may be summed up in the remark attributed to W. G. Grace (apocryphal or not) when bowled by an unknown in a charity match: 'They came to see me bat, not to see you bowl', proceeding to trounce the unfortunate trundler. Not that the counties failed to nurture their best bowlers as well as their best batsmen. Lancashire rejoiced at the recovery (alas! so fleeting) of Briggs because they needed him as a bowler much more

now than a batsman. Certainly to support the powerful batting—
even in the temporary and much lamented absence of Spooner, on
duty with the Militia in Ireland—the side had much bowling
strength, with Sharp and Webb to back up Briggs and Mold.

Briggs, so near the end of his career and his life, achieved his
greatest bowling triumph, to the unrestrained joy of his innumerable fans to whom he was a hero even as a bowler or fielder—at
Old Trafford. In Worcestershire's first innings there he took all ten
wickets for 55 runs in 28·5 overs, 7 of them maidens. This great
performance outshone other feats with both bat and ball, a number
of which that eventful summer, were far from inconsiderable,
MacLaren hit 102 in 75 minutes at Southampton and Hartley 109
in 110 minutes at Glossop. Mold took 12 wickets for 46 runs at
Hastings, but disaster was soon afterwards to overwhelm him.
That nagging criticism of 'suspect' actions had been mounting in
volume and there seems no doubt from the weight of contemporary
evidence that Mold sometimes threw.

At any rate, accusing fingers pointed in his direction and, at Old
Trafford that summer he was no-balled by umpire James Phillips,
an Australian who had a reputation for toughness and had previously 'called' Ernest Jones in Australia. He also no-balled C. B.
Fry of Sussex and Tyler of Somerset. For Mold it was the beginning of the end. He was left out of the side and had the mortifi-
cation of watching his own benefit match, against Yorkshire, from a
seat. But his benefit, more than £2,000, was the highest recorded
up to that time. That winter the county captains drew up two
lists, one of bowlers to be barred altogether—C. B. Fry, Capt.
Bradford, Griffin, Mold, F. Davidson, Rooke, W. G. Quaife and
Geeson—and one of those to be warned (H. G. Bull, Tyler, Bland
and Lockwood). Lancashire challenged the authority of the captains and played Mold in 1901. But when Lancashire met Somerset
Phillips was again the umpire. There was an ominous silence when
Phillips first no-balled Mold but, as he continued to 'call' him
(the final tally of no-balls was eighteen) the fury of the crowd
broke. Police protection had to be sought for Phillips. The protests,
widespread and angry as they were, did not avail. Mold that day
was no-balled out of cricket. Like many others in the sides of
those days (and quite a few in these, come to that) he was not
'pure' Lancashire. He was born within the boundary of Northants
and played a few times for that county before joining Lancashire in

1889, earning himself almost instant fame by grabbing thirteen Yorkshire wickets. In 1892 he was one of *Wisden*'s 'Five Great Bowlers'. In 259 matches for the county he had taken 1,541 wickets at a cost of 15·13 each and hit 1,669 runs averaging 7·13 an innings.

Mold took his eclipse philosophically. His main complaint, put forward in a reasonably judicial manner, was that he should have been stopped at the beginning of his career, for his greatest feats could only be diminished by the ban. Controversy rumbled on. It was claimed that ciné shots of Mold in the nets at Lords (surely the first of such recordings) showed that there was 'not a suggestion of a throw in his action'. But the Editor of *Wisden* was firmly of the other opinion. He wrote: 'Knowing, as I do, the opinions expressed in private by several of the greatest batsmen in the country, I regard Mold as the luckiest of men to have gone through a dozen seasons without being no-balled.' Phillips made many enemies but he certainly had the courage to back his convictions. Long after Phillips' death, C. B. Fry, discussing this great chucking row, said of him: 'He was not a bad sort but obstinate to a degree.'

Altogether, the season of 1901 was far from happy for Lancashire, Cuttell broke a bone in his hand and Briggs suffered the final breakdown which led to his death early the following year. As a result Lancashire lost three stalwarts, all Test players, and, in the circumstances did well to finish third in the championship table. In addition to trouble with the stars, there was much trouble with the pitch. During the winter inadequately sieved dressing was applied to it, the result being the appearance of small pebbles which had been rolled into the turf.

On such a wicket fast bowlers were a double menace. C. J. Kortright, perhaps the fastest of his day, bowled on it near-lethal flyers, one of which knocked out Johnny Tyldesley. Not that the blow achieved much for the visitors. Tyldesley returned heavily bandaged to give Kortright 'a proper belting'. MacLaren was furious about the state of the square. On one occasion he marched into the Committee Room at Old Trafford and flung a handful of pebbles down on the table. Nobody seems quite able to pin down the occasion but it could have been after Hirst, bowling at a terrific pace, had bounced Lancashire out for 44 (his match figures were 12 for 70) and, defying the conditions, he was the only batsman to reach 40. Referring to that wicked wicket years later Sir Neville

Cardus wrote that it 'imperiled kneecap, breast-bone and Adam's apple alike'.

A wet spell and a lot of labour finally righted the villainous strip with a resultant upsurge in run-amassing. Tyldesley, who had a truly prolific season, topping 3,000 runs in all games, and H. G. Garnett, put on 148 runs in 80 minutes in a gallant but unavailing bid to hit 307 runs in four hours against Sussex after Ranji had scored 69 and 170 not out. Garnett's share of the glut was 110 and 89. J. T. Broughton, who played in only 6 matches for Lancashire, had the distinction, tinged with melancholy, of hitting 99 in his first game, against Essex.

As the season ended, MacLaren caused some consternation by announcing that he must give up the captaincy as he intended to go south, for his wife's health, and play for Hampshire.

The method used to make the announcement—by means of a letter from the county Secretary to the Press—was criticised but not nearly as heavily as was MacLaren's choice (and it was his alone) of S. F. Barnes to go to Australia that winter under his captaincy. Barnes then, as for so long later, was a League player. He had appeared for Warwickshire, taking 13 wickets in all, and for Lancashire, for which side he had taken but 3 wickets until the last match of the season. This was against Leicestershire and Barnes, fast medium, with a short run-up, high action and perfect balance, opened the bowling with slow left-hander Webb. In 29 overs, of which 7 were maidens, Barnes took 6 wickets for 70 runs.

After the game Albert Ward asked him: 'Has MacLaren said anything about going to Australia?' Barnes thought it was a leg-pull—and when the invitation did turn up he did not at once reply. He was playing in his League team when his captain, Joe Allan, heard about it. He ordered Barnes to leave the field at once and accept. When the team for Australia was announced the Press roared 'Who's Barnes?' and MacLaren, whose judgment was not always sound to say the least of it, had to put up with a sustained barrage. Even Barnes himself was dubious. He had never even seen a Test match and had certainly never imagined playing in one. He told MacLaren that he did not consider himself a fast bowler. 'You are fast enough for what I want,' MacLaren replied. As it turned out MacLaren's hunch was amply justified.

Sydney Barnes had proved himself a bowler of Test class and

was, in fact, hailed as the best English bowler seen in Australia up to then. In the Test matches he took 19 wickets averaging 17 runs each and then developed knee trouble which, some of his contemporaries claimed, deprived us of the chance of regaining the Ashes. Barnes returned home with an established reputation. Subsequently, though he transferred from first class to Minor County cricket, then went back to the League, he won a place in the gallery of Test immortals, taking 189 wickets in 27 Tests which kept him at the top of the Test bowlers list for many years (heading Maurice Tate, with 155 wickets in 39 Tests) until overhauled by Trueman, Statham, Bedser and Laker.

His average, 16·43 per wicket, remains to this day the lowest of all, apart from G. A. Lohmann, of Surrey (18 Tests, 112 wickets, average 10·75). And still he holds the record for the most wickets in a Test rubber, 49 (at 10·93 each) v. South Africa in 1913–14. This record was achieved in only four games and included 17 wickets for 159 runs at Johannesburg. His personal relationship with Lancashire authorities was never entirely easy. Afer his success in Australia Barnes became a regular member of the Lancashire side. At Old Trafford one day he was summoned to the Committee Room where the Secretary handed him a letter from the M.C.C. warning the County to be careful what they did about Barnes 'because we know he is not qualified for Lancashire'. Barnes retorted that he was as much qualified as some others he knew.

The Committee decided to play him and see what happened, and later he did qualify. His knee was still troubling him but, nevertheless, that season he took 82 wickets averaging 21, bowling more overs than any other member of the team. Barnes had the somewhat depressing experience of being boo-ed when he appeared on the field at Sheffield to play in his first home Test match, against Australia. But this hostile demonstration was not so much *against* him as *for* Schofield Haigh, of Yorkshire, whom he had supplanted. His reply to his critics was an analysis of 6 for 49.

He was not chosen for the famous Old Trafford Test, a decision directly responsible for the catastrophe which overwhelmed poor Fred Tate and, in the opinion of many, for England's defeat. This Test was historic not only for Tate's dropped catch but for swiftly changing fortunes and shining feats among which the innings of Australia's Victor Trumper stood out, and stands out still, for sheer, breathless brilliance. It was, indeed, one of the most thrilling,

narrowly won-and-lost games in all cricket at all times. The
Selectors, it has been widely accepted, blundered in triplicate—in
picking Lionel Palairet instead of all-rounder Hirst, in not choosing
Jessop the mighty, and in playing Tate instead of Barnes. The
wicket was soft and easy-paced. Darling, captain of the Australian
team, almost certainly the best sent over here up to that date, won
the toss.

Trumper and Duff opened the Australian innings and, at lunch
time on the first day, the score was 173. Trumper had hit a century,
the first before lunch in any Test. His score stood at 103, a remarkable feat considering that the outfield was sluggish and even
muddy. His pulling was bold and powerful and those who were
there to glory in Trumper's absolute mastery declared for long years
afterwards that this was the greatest innings of all time. Trumper
was out, for 104, soon after the interval, after which only Darling
dealt firmly with Lockwood, to hit a lusty 51 in the tourists's total
of 299. MacLaren was once more in the firing line—for not having
put Lockwood on sooner than he did. The score was 129 for 0
when he was called upon and promptly he took Duff's wicket. Tate
bowled, but without success.

England replied with 262, to which F. S. Jackson contributed
128, an innings proclaimed to be the best in all his lustrous Test
career. When he and Len Braund came together England were
44 for 5. They put on 122 invaluable runs, Braund's share being
65. Johnny Tyldesley was third highest scorer, with 22. This great
stand evened up the game once more, but it swung dramatically in
England's favour when the Australians had lost Trumper, Duff and
Hill, all Lockwood's victims, for 10 runs in their second innings.
Darling and Gregory were now together. Doggedly, they raised the
total to 16. It was at this breath-taking stage in the proceedings that
MacLaren made another disastrous error. He sent Tate, a close-in
fielder out of his element in the 'country', into the deep on the leg
side to replace Palairet, brought up to short leg at the request of
bowler Braund.

Darling hit the ball hard and high. Tate, unused to such a
position, misjudged it and dropped the catch. Darling and
Gregory then put on 54 runs, enough to win the match by the
incredibly narrow margin of three runs, and to retain the Ashes.
Braund subsequently described the sad episode thus: 'I was bowling to Syd Gregory and, after the fifth ball of the over he played me

wide of mid-off for a single, which brought Joe Darling, a left-hander, down for the last ball. I said to Mr MacLaren, "Can I have Mr Palairet across to square leg?" (that was the position in which he fielded to Braund in the Somerset team, knowing the curve of the ball when a left hander hit Braund's leg break). MacLaren said 'What, do you want me to ask Lionel Palairet to run right across Old Trafford for one ball? Send Fred Tate out there". And he did. Surely enough Joe Darling carted me next ball with the spin, high out to leg, and it curved as it always does when a left hander hits the leg break with the spin, poor Fred Tate moved to his right and then, as it boomeranged away, tried to get back, got his left hand to it but dropped it—there it was—I had to come off.'

In spite of this 'bonus' stand Australia were all out for 86 and, when MacLaren and Palairet had scored 36 before lunch an England victory looked certain. Palairet was out soon after the resumption of play but MacLaren and Abel scored briskly so that the total had reached 92 (at which point nobody would have put a tizzy on the Aussies) when the fourth wicket fell.

MacLaren, indeed, had had to face a rebuke from Ranji for hitting out recklessly enough to lose his wicket, being caught in the long field. As he returned to the pavilion Ranji said (according to that faithful chronicler Howard) 'Whatever did you do that for?' The captain of England and Lancashire steered Ranji to the balcony and said severely: 'Can't you see the rain coming? That's the reason.' It was certainly a lowering sky beneath which tension mounted as Trumble and Saunders, in a devastating spell of bowling, dismissed Jackson, Braund, Abel and Lockwood for 17 runs. Rhodes and wicket-keeper Lilley made some good strokes but with England needing eight runs to win Lilley, seeking to satisfy this requirement without too much delay, was brilliantly caught on the square leg boundary by Clem Hill, running at top speed. Eight to win and the last man in . . . Tate, praying to retrieve himself, acutely conscious of his unenviable position as England's last hope, walked out to the wicket and stood, far from at ease, at one end while Rhodes played out the over. Then that heavy rain MacLaren had anticipated, descended from the dark sky. Tate returned to the dressing room there to sit with his pads on, bat between his knees, the fate of England on his shoulders, for forty-five of the longest minutes in any man's story. There was no shortage of advice. At last the rain eased and the representatives of Yorkshire and of Sussex walked with apparent composure, to the wicket. Australian morale was now high, tension all round the ground higher still. Left arm bowler Saunders, exuding confidence after luring to destruction rather better batsmen, bowled round the wicket to England's last man in. Tate stabbed down in the first ball, which flew off the edge of his bat down to fine leg for four. The cheering had a hysterical quality. Then a tense, dense, silence . . . Four to win . . . Tate survived the next two balls. The fourth, rather faster, with the arm and keeping low, bowled him. Whether it was an in-swinger as has often been claimed or, as William Howard bluntly put it a 'shooter', matters little. It was unplayable by Tate and would have been unplayable by a good many far better batsmen. It was, in any case, decisive. The Australians had won the most exciting of all Test matches—at any rate up to the classic Australia-West Indies tie (in 1960–61)—by three runs, and with them held on to the Ashes. Tate, normally the most affable of men, plump enough to be known as 'Chubby' or 'Chub', was inconsolable. But on the way home to Sussex he recovered sufficiently to confide in Len Braund: 'I've got a little kid there at home who'll make up for it to me.' The little kid was Maurice Tate (another 'Chub') who may be said to have done just that. The two characters best remembered among that *Dramatis Personnae* of that finest game of cricket in Old Trafford's history had splendid records that summer. Despite wretched weather Trumper made 2,570 runs, including eleven centuries, averaging 48, and earned from *Wisden* the encomium: 'Trumper stood alone among batsmen of the season.' Fred Tate took 180 wickets at 15 runs apiece.

Yorkshire, champions for the third year running, crushed Lancashire at Bramall Lane, winning by an innings after Barnes had seen them out for only 148. Stanley Jackson, on a treacherous wicket, took 8 wickets for 13 (3 for 5 ad 5 for 8) and scored 33. At Old Trafford scoring was prolific. For Yorkshire Denton and Hirst hit not out centuries, Jackson 80, Tunnicliffe, Taylor and Irving Washington half centuries. Lancashire were saved only by what in insurance claims may be termed 'an act of God', Manchester's relentless rain.

A young man with a great future made an inauspicious debut as a fast bowler. His name was Walter Brearley. However he was to make far greater impact in the summer (a technical term, it was

said to be the worst, climatically, since the start of the championship) of 1903. He took 125 wickets and endeared himself to Lancastrians everywhere by dismissing six Yorkshiremen in the second
innings of the drawn game at Old Trafford. Barnes improved
greatly on his performance of the previous year, taking 131 championship wickets, averaging 17 runs each. By now he had developed
the leg break which was to claim many a hapless victim. To the
dismay of all good Lancastrians, not over-sensitive about the fact
that he was, so to speak, 'naturalised', Barnes's slightly scratchy
relationship with the Committee degenerated over financial matters
—he wanted long term security they were unprepared to concede—
and he left the county.

However, bygones can be bygones as Barnes proved when he returned to Old Trafford 30 years later as coach, the action just as
high to extract a youthfully kicking bounce from the pitch, though
he was sixty. Was there ever a better bowler on all types of wickets?
Many there were among his contemporaries who thought he was
the best of all and there are some who will make the assertion
today. The late Denzil Batchelor (in *The Book of Cricket*) was
emphatic on the point. He wrote: 'Tall, with a high action, and
every ball from out-swinger to leg-break under his command, he
is the bowler against whom Australians and South Africans will
measure your latter day genius—and find that the newcomer falls
short. Never was such a perfect length! Never was such a kick off
the wicket from a fast-medium bowler! Never was such a devilish
ball cutting in from the on to invite the dolly catch to the leg field
. . .' He seemed to be capable of bowling whatever ball he chose
whenever he wanted to. He once, very matily, cautioned a batsman: 'If thee don't get thy left foot across I'm going to bowl you
between your legs and the bat.' He did.

8 *Bowl-All-Day Brearley*

The year that Barnes left Lancashire, for his native county—he was born in Smethwick—was significant in Manchester's, and England's social history for a determined step in the direction of feminine emancipation. Mrs Pankhurst, who was to become world-famous as a Suffragette leader, founded in Manchester the Women's Social and Political Union; later a secessionist group formed the Women's Freedom League. And while the women of England were beginning to assert themselves, the cricketers of Lancashire were asserting themselves too. Lancashire, despite gloomy auspices which included grave doubts about the bowling following the loss of Mold, Briggs, Barnes and Hallam (who had transferred himself to Nottingham) had an unexpected runaway triumph in 1904. They were outstanding champions, winning six matches more than the runners-up, Kent, and seven more than Yorkshire, placed third. They did not lose a single game, winning 16 out of 26. The weather, and the general strength of batting, accounted for the high proportion of drawn games. Lancashire's batsmen were high among the run-getters in this, their peak year of the Golden Age of Batsmanship. Two Australians played their parts in the success of this side, young and old players fusing to form one of the most formidable combinations in the county's history.

They were Alexander Kermode, a big, burly fast bowler who had been spotted by MacLaren in New South Wales and prevailed upon to come over, and Dr L. O. S. Poidevin, who studied medicine here and settled in Manchester. The old guard gave the team a fine start with an innings win over Leicester. Spooner and Garnett hit 137 in 80 minutes and Cuttell bowled with dash and accuracy to clinch matters, initiating, incidentally, an astonishing come-back which guided him to the bowler's goal, 100 wickets, at the age of forty. James Hallows, from near Bolton, uncle of the more famous Charles Hallows, in his 30th year achieved the 'double'. He was a

left-hand bat of much grace and a left-hand bowler of much guile.
He might have earned much more fame but for poor health which
led to his early death, at 34. Brearley, immensely energetic and
zestful—'a gale of humanity' was the picturesque description
applied to him by Sir Neville Cardus— dominated the first match at
Old Trafford where Warwickshire were beaten by nine wickets.
His contribution was a match analysis of 12 wickets for 144 runs;
Spooner and Tyldesley hit off the last 80 runs in three quarters of
an hour, not perhaps, such a remarkable feat then as it would be
today.

Brearley, one of the fittest men of his or any other generation,
was virtually tireless. He would willingly bowl all day and, indeed,
hated to be taken off. There is an old story which, strictly true or
not typifies him. It runs:

'Well, Walter, shall we have a change?'

'Yes, skipper, I will go on at the other end.'

He had a tricky run which started with a disconcerting quick-
step to the left and developed into a sailor-like roll. The ball, fast
through the air, was even faster off the ground. He has been described as the most hostile bowler between F. R. Spofforth, the
'demon' from Australia, and Fred Trueman. At any rate his zest
was vast, unquenchable. He could not get out there quickly
enough, often vaulting the rails in his eagerness to get at the opposition. This demonstration of agility he would make even when
going out to bat, an aspect of the game in which his enthusiasm
outran his ability.

Once, and once only, it seemed possible that he was on his way
to a half century. The match was against Sussex in that 1904
season. With half an hour to play and eight Lancashire wickets
down, Sussex seemed less than anxious to bat overnight and the
bowling was not formidable. Brearley was 27 not out at the close
and readily accepted the long odds his captain offered against the
fifty he now confidently expected to score. The next morning he
was at the ground early and, as William Howard recalled, he batted
longer in the nets than normally he did in a whole season. Alas!
he was given out, caught, in the first over. For once he was motion-
less, and speechless. When he realised that the umpire had given
him out he returned, dejected, to the dressing room, announcing
that he would later tell the Sussex players what he thought of
them. This he did. He also had a few words to utter when a Kent

A. N. 'Monkey' Hornby, dashing batsman and fearless fielder, captain of
Lancashire 1880–91, 1892–3 (joint) and
1897–8.

Archie MacLaren, one of the greatest
of Lancashire captains and a stylish
batsman—he played 35 times for
England.

R. G. Barlow, Hornby's partner for
Lancashire on so many occasions, an
excellent field and a first class left-
hand bowler.

Johnny Briggs, fine all-rounder and
rare character, whose end was tragic.

J. T. Tyldesley, one of the greatest and most attractive of Lancashire batsmen. He scored 1,000 runs in a season 19 times.

The Lancashire team of 1894, *L to r*: Standing—Mold, Paul, Lunt (scorer), Baker Smith (A); sitting—Ward (A), S. M. Tindall, A. C. MacLaren (capt.), G. R Bardswell, Sugg; front—Briggs, Smith (C), Tinsley.

Old Trafford group in the late Twenties: *L to r*: J. T. Tyldesley, Sir Edwin Stockton, Reg Parkin and his father, the inimitable Cecil Parkin.

Charlie Hallows batting against the Australians at Old Trafford in 1926. Bert Oldfield is the wicketkeeper.

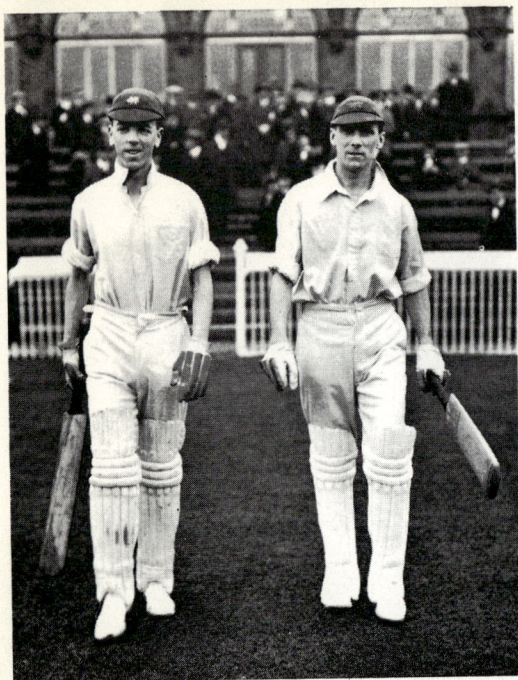

Hopwood and Hallows, going out to open for Lancashire at Old Trafford—a formidable pair in some of the County's greatest years.

Smiles in the Old Trafford rain! *L to r*: Richard Tyldesley, the young George Duckworth, Watson, Green, Harry Makepeace and Ernest Tyldesley. The year—1926.

Lancashire's greatest ever fast bowlers: (top) E. A. McDonald, the superbly hostile Australian, and (bottom) Brian Statham whose control and skill have never been surpassed.

The George Duckworth appeal in action—and Surrey's Laurie Fishlock looks suitably impressed!

Cyril Washbrook, Lancashire's first professional captain, in action. For both England and the County he was a tower of strength.

One of Jim Laker's fantastic 19 wickets in the Old Trafford Test v. Australia, 1956.
Keith Miller caught by Alan Oakman in the first innings.

At the end of that amazing match the crowd erupted to pay tribute to a bowling
feat that is hardly likely to be repeated.

Two of the players who played a vital part in Lancashire's great revival at the close of the Sixties: (left) West Indian Clive Lloyd and (below) Jack Bond, a really inspiring captain.

bowler hit him on the head with a bouncer, the ball proceeding to the boundary and Brearley to the turf, out for the count. He soon recovered his senses and his invective.

Golden Age batsmanship was nobly exemplified when Lancashire met Sussex upon the occasion when Brearley nearly achieved batting fame. The two most dazzling pairs in all England both displayed their brilliance, Spooner and MacLaren sending up 200 in less than two hours, Fry defying the Lancashire bowlers with a lustrous century and Ranji with a half century of poetic artistry. MacLaren and Tyldesley and bowlers Sharp and Cuttell, all hit centuries off Somerset, the first two recording 187 together in 105 minutes—in a total of 580; they also ran up 324 together against Notts. Tyldesley was irrepressible. He hit 196 off the Worcestershire bowlers and, with Spooner, knocked up 166 in 100 minutes against Essex. The season which had started with such forebodings ended with one of the finest, best balanced sides in all the Lancashire annals. This was the order for the Champions v. the Rest of England match: A. C. MacLaren, R. H. Spooner, J. T. Tyldesley, L. O. S. Poidevin, H. G. Garnett, J. Hallows, W. R. Cuttell, J. l'Anson, W. Findlay (later Secretary of the M.C.C.), A. Kermode. Brearley, to the dismay of his fans and his own manifest wrath, was dropped. At once he announced his retirement. However, he was persuaded to think again and was to be observed leaping into the Old Trafford playing area with all his old verve at the start of the 1905 season. Lancashire failed to retain the championship but put up an inspiring fight for it.

They might well have tied for the championship had it not been for the presence of the Australians, once more under the captaincy of Joe Darling. When Lancashire played Gloucestershire a draw would have ensured that half share. But in the absence, playing for England, of MacLaren, Spooner, Brearley and Tyldesley, they lost.

As in 1902 so in 1905 the Old Trafford Test was decisive but this time it was England who, under F. S. Jackson (he had replaced MacLaren as captain) retained the Ashes. And Spooner, to the delight of the Manchester crowd, was associated in one of the most glorious partnerships of the year, 125 with Jackson, who hit a century and was to emerge from the series not only victorious but at the top of both the batting and the bowling averages. England, batting first (to Darling's dismay Jacker won the toss in all five

Tests) easily beat Australia, batting after rain and hounded by
Brearley at his ferocious best.

Brearley and Kermode had to bear the brunt of the bowling for
Lancashire that season, Cuttell having lost his form (and his place)
and Hallows his effectiveness. But for the batting there was still no
county to touch them. Nine of the team had averages over 20 with
Poidevin, who hit five hundreds, at the top. Brearley had a re-
markable record at Old Trafford. Against Somerset he took 9
wickets for 47 runs and the West countrymen were all out for 65.
It was, indeed, a day's cricket unique in the county championship.
At close of play Lancashire were 424 with two wickets standing.
Lancashire's score, in the last forty minutes leapt by 139, A. H.
Hornby's share being 93.

He completed his century the next morning and brought the ninth
wicket stand with wicket-keeper Findlay up to 113 in half an hour.
For Brearley it was a match never to be forgotten. His aggregate of
17 wickets included four with four successive balls. After this
personal triumph it was, perhaps, unfortunate that Brearley should
have been in the centre of bitterly angry scenes on the Old Trafford
ground. Gloucestershire were the visitors and Brearley, not the
easiest of characters, took umbrage at some leg-pulling about his
batting, which was hardly in the classic mould whatever his own
assessment of it. One jest riled him especially. Ill feeling flared,
and when Gloucester were in an apparently hopeless position at
47 for 3 Jessop the mighty, Gloucester's captain, and Board,
started to hit out at everything offered to them. Brearley, still
smarting, sought to stem the tidal wave by bowling full tosses at
the batsmen's heads. Jessop and Broad contemptuously slogged
57 runs off four overs, 98 runs in 40 minutes. Ultimately Brearley
got them both out and the roughest match ever staged at Old
Trafford ended, amidst unprecedented acrimony, in a Lancashire
victory.

Jessop threatened never to play there again and publicly criticised
Walter Brearley. But the breach was eventually healed. The most
bewildered man at Old Trafford that turbulent day was, undoubtedly, 23-years-old Billy Cook from Preston, playing in his
first county match. He had a splendid start to a brief career, taking
11 wickets, but he must have wondered whether county cricket
could possibly offer a congenial occupation.

A happier atmosphere prevailed on the occasion of the Roses

match. On Whit Monday 25,000 people were amply rewarded by the magnificence of Spooner and Tyldesley, who put on 253 for the second wicket, a dazzling display of all-round batsmanship said by many present to be the finest on that famous ground. Fast scoring enlivened a less lustrous season the following year when Lancashire suffered from the frequent absence of Brearley and MacLaren. The Kent fixture at Old Trafford provided a notable example. Lancashire scored 531 at the rate of 100 runs an hour, Johnny Tyldesley hitting 295 of them. More significant in cricket history was the debut of Frank Woolley. It was not an auspicious start to one of the greatest careers of all. Young Woolley muffed two catches, failed to score and had 103 runs hit off his bowling for the capture of one wicket. However, in Kent's second innings he showed more than a glimpse of the grace and power he was to display for many years. Kent, that year, won the championship.

Once more Spooner touched the heights, hitting a century before lunch against Somerset and proceeding to 240 majestic runs in 260 fleeting minutes. He and Jimmy Heap, a left arm bowler and useful bat, put on 114 in one hour against Worcestershire. Tyldesley maintained his place in the fast scoring race with 102 in 80 minutes off the Warwickshire bowlers. Willis Cuttell, in his last season, displayed some of his old form. In fact he finished second in the national bowling averages though with only 65 wickets.

Ahead of him was another Lancashire player. Huddleston, a medium pacer whose aggregate of wickets was even more modest, 52. At any rate the pair set up a new Lancashire record—never before had two Lancashire men headed the list. Both Roses matches were lost, the second, at Old Trafford, due largely to the bowling of Rhodes and Haigh. MacLaren, with an uncharacteristically crude stroke which betrayed exasperation, hit his own wicket. An illustrious name was seen for the first time in the upper half of the batting order, Harry Makepeace.

The next summer brought little distinction to Lancashire, the side descending to sixth place in the championship. A newcomer who was to become one of Lancashire's characters and command tremendous fan loyalty made a modest bow—Lawrence Cook, soon to be known as 'Lol', brother of Billy Cook. He proved to be one of the most loyal and hard-working cricketers Lancashire had —and it had many with these virtues. He was a 'natural' for holding up an end if necessary for hours, though his off-break could and did cause the greatest batsmen trouble—even Jack Hobbs. It was said of 'Lol' Cook that he kept as immaculate a length as did Alfred Shaw, a compliment indeed. Like Maurice Tate in later years he was permanently convinced that the gods were against him. His anguished high-decibel appeals could be heard over wide areas; his supplications to heaven at the cruel absence of that extra coat of varnish robbing him of a certain wicket, wrung innumerable withers.

The most memorable episode of this year was scarcely felicitous. At Lord's, rain—as heavy as any Manchester could boast—ended play on the first day when the Lancashire score stood at 57 for 1 wicket. The second day was blank and, after the umpires' decision had been announced, a few disgruntled spectators decided to inspect the pitch themselves. Great argument ensued. It involved the two captains, the umpires and the players. At the end of it MacLaren issued a statement to the Press which read: '*Owing to the pitch having been deliberately torn up by the public, I, as captain of the Lancashire Eleven, cannot see my way to continue the game, the groundsmen bearing me out that the wicket could not be again put right.—A. C. MacLaren*'.

The Middlesex President, R. D. Walker (brother of V. E.) also communicated his views to the Press, stating that when the pitch was rolled the following morning the damage was reduced to one rather deep heel mark. It was MacLaren's last protest as captain of Lancashire though he did subsequently again captain England. He skippered the team for the last time in the last match of the season—which resulted in a dramatic two wickets win over Leicestershire—then handed over to A. H. Hornby. Brilliant, unpredictable, often dreaming up bright but impracticable ideas (such as pneumatic pads) capable of being so right about Barnes, so wrong as to stop that Lord's match, he could look back upon triumphs and tribulations, adulation and condemnation.

Like many other great players and, in particular, controversial captains, he had had to put up with much criticism, even abuse, so fanatical was cricket's following in the 'Golden Age'. After that unforgettable 1902 Test, MacLaren received a postcard photograph of a gang of workmen, with the suggestion that they would do the old country credit in the last Test at the Oval 'as the old fogies seem to be suffering from nerves.' And, when Lancashire were decisively beaten by Warwickshire in 1901 a wooden box addressed to the Lancashire team arrived at Old Trafford—from South Africa. Inside was a skilfully made mini-coffin inscribed 'In memory of the Lancashire C.C.C. who died, 5th June 1901'.

More personal, however, was a postcard received by MacLaren. It read: 'The young ladies of Miss Cranmar's Seminary desire to challenge you and your merry men to a game of bobber and kibs on our ground near the *Marble Arch-ie* to take place, say, on next All *Hallows* Eve. Don't be afraid to take us on, we won't hurt you. Should you be *Sharp* enough to win we will *A-Ward* you a free repast, consisting of *Eccles* cakes and *Hartleys* jam. *Do* come, we beseech you. By the way, might we suggest that you alter the name of the approach to the County Ground. Warwick Road is too painfully suggestive.' With the pun rampant at the time, all those italics drawing attention to this form of humour would seem to be superflous.

Another 'wit' wrote to MacLaren: On the Monday prior to the Whitsuntide festival next season, kindly present each possible player of the side selected to represent Lancashire v Yorkshire with one bottle of Yorkshire relish as an antidote to Yorkshire Paralysis.'

Whatever his shortcomings MacLaren was a zestful character. After cricket, his greatest sporting interest, was perhaps, racing—he was at one time a racehorse owner. When Old Trafford lived right up to (or down to) its climatic reputation during the Kent match in 1904 it was decided to spend the second day, which was washed out, at Manchester Races. It would seem that the Lancashire captain was not out of pocket for, at the end of the day, he said to one of the Kent players, with the somewhat ponderously pawky humour he sometimes displayed: 'There is no chance whatever of finishing the match; we might just as well get someone to pour water on the wicket all night and we can get to the races again tomorrow.'

This was not feasible as play was resumed. Kent players might well have preferred the races. They were put out twice and Lancashire won with half an hour to spare.

MacLaren is not the subject of so many anecdotes as some of the more flamboyant of his contemporaries. This was partly due, no doubt, to the fact that so often so much depended on him. One story certainly illustrates this point. A Lancashire player, watching the disintegration of his side murmured: 'If only Archie could get someone to stay with him'. To which prayer a dear old lady among those present, replied: 'Dear me, is he as unpopular with the team as all that!'

Archie MacLaren was one of those immortal exemplars whose cricketing image continued to exert its potent influence long after his departure from the game, down to generations unborn in his era. He was virtually certain of a place in those Titanic tide-to-tide 'Tests' in which I participated on the sands of Sussex in the 1920s (though I was usually W.G., being the fortunate possessor of an awesome-looking property beard). And, only recently, from cricket's upper echelons, came another example of MacLaren's long-range influence. My old friend and cricketing companion Denis Castle was having a jar at the end of a summer's day with Andy Sandham, illustrious Surrey partner and lifelong friend of Jack Hobbs, when the latter asked: 'Who did you pretend you were when you played cricket as a small boy?' Replied Denis: 'Hobbs', adding tactfully, 'but sometimes you.' Said Sandy with feeling: 'I was *always* MacLaren.'

Under the new skipper, Hornby the Second, Brearley bowled with all his old verve to take 148 inexpensive wickets in only 17 championship matches, earning himself a place among *Wisden's* 'Five Cricketers of the Year'. Huddleston, the most successful bowler after Brearley and Dean, found himself in the odd position of being regarded as a soft wicket bowler, left out if the going was hard. He was not picked for the Kent fixture at Tunbridge Wells but, when it was perceived that the wicket might help him he was summoned by telegram to travel south. He responded to this S.O.S. with 4 for 38 in Kent's first innings.

There was little reason to clamour for brighter cricket. When Lancashire played Somerset the west countrymen had the best of the first innings. Then Lancashire, and in particular Sharp, Tyldesley and MacLaren, hit 400 runs at 100 runs an hour. Following this glut, Brearley and Dean disposed of Somerset in 50 minutes for 33 runs, the former claiming 5 wickets for 14 runs. Lancashire rose to second place the next season, beating Surrey twice and Kent, who emerged as the champion county, once. One of the most exciting games of the season was notable for the fact that centuries were scored by two Rugby internationals. John Daniell hit one for Somerset and Ken McLeod's 128 in only 95 minutes enabled Lancashire to win by 9 runs with just 5 minutes left for play.

Revenge for that coffin-inspiring defeat by Warwickshire earlier in the century was sweet indeed. Hornby sent Warwick in to bat and Dean took 9 wickets for 35 runs; in the second innings he added to this total 4 for 46 and Huddleston had 6 for 19. But the most significant aspect of the match, played early in June, was the first appearance of Ernest Tyldesley, younger brother of J.T., whose form had declined—temporarily as it happily turned out. To Johnny's delight Ernest scored 61, taking part in one of those crowd-thrilling, fast-scoring partnerships for which Lancashire were noted, putting on 128 runs in 90 minutes with MacLaren. Ironical was the outcome of a change in the method of assessing places in the championship table in 1910. Lancashire suggested the alteration in the interests of simplification.

The determining figure became the percentage of wins to matches played. Under the previous system Lancashire would have been runners-up; under the new they were fourth. The disappointment caused by a large number of drawn games due to rain, 10 out of 29 played (one, against Kent, was cut to two days because of the funeral of King Edward VII) was offset by some remarkable feats, including two 'impossible' victories each involving the scoring of more than 400 runs in the fourth innings. The first, at Old Trafford, established a new record in first-class cricket. Nottinghamshire had dominated the game, scoring 376 in the first innings, helped by a Hardstaff century, and then dismissed Lancashire for 162. Lancashire's defeat looked a certainty but A. O. Jones, the Notts captain, decided not to enforce the follow-on, a fatal decision as his batsmen wasted hours prodding away at funereal pace. On the third day, in something like panic, 8 wickets were thrown away for 45 runs in an attempt to force the pace. Lancashire were left with $5\frac{1}{4}$ hours in which to score 400 runs, a last innings total never before realised. They set about the task with gusto. John Tyldesley, back to form, with 91 and Sharp (102) put on 191 runs in 150 minutes; then Ernest Tyldesley and Whitehead increased even this brisk pace to add 80 runs in 40 minutes. But, with more than 80 runs still wanted and only two wickets to fall Lancashire were behind the clock and hardly 'fancied—especially as skipper Hornby, the only remaining hope, was injured.

When he walked out to bat the crowd was unaware of the drama within the drama which had been enacted inside the pavilion. Hornby had been suffering cartilage trouble for a long time and his loose cartilage had become displaced while fielding. As he could scarcely hobble he had put himself in last. The extraordinary restoration of Hornby was described by William Howard (who played an important part) in his autobiography thus: 'Going to the bar for a small soda, or something to relieve the excitement, I met one of our old members, John Allison, who seldom came to see a match, and, judging by his appearance, was celebrating this occasion. He was the proprietor of a nursing home in Manchester, and was well respected by all who knew him. Answering his inquiries about Mr Hornby, I informed him of the state of affairs, and, to my astonishment, Mr Allison insisted on going into the dressing-room, determined to make the Lancashire captain fit to bat. It was useless to remonstrate, so I reluctantly took him up. Five minutes later Mr Hornby had his pads on, ready to go in at the fall of the next wicket. Our friend, who was responsible for the transformation, looked quite elated with his success. It was a most lucky thing for Lancashire, especially as it happened at an opportune moment; two wickets falling quickly about this time had made the prospects of victory seem bad.

'When Mr Hornby went in, still suffering from pain, over eighty runs were wanted and the clock against us. Eight men out, thirty-six to win, when Lol Cook joined his captain—excitement intense. Two minutes from time Lancashire won a magnificent match by two wickets, Mr Hornby scoring 55 not out, a plucky and resolute innings. He was carried shoulder high off the ground, the crowd singing "For he's a jolly good fellow". Long after the match was over, Mr Allison called me to the refreshment bar to confirm what he had repeatedly told his friends; that it was he who won the match.'

Hornby had a strong sense of the captain's responsibility. If there were only a few minutes left for play and a wicket fell he would go in himself rather than thrust an unpopular situation on somebody else. As a fielder he was as courageous as his father had been—perhaps more reckless. He would stand at 'suicide' silly point, even to a hitter, which 'put the wind up' Howard, as he confessed. 'Hornby in jeopardy,' he would say.

Lancashire had, in fact, scored 403 in that historic innings and that proved to be exactly the total needed to beat Hampshire later in the season—but in only five hours. Hartley and another Tyldesley, W., gave Lancashire a fabulous start with 100 runs in one hour, then Sharp and Makepeace, often partners on the soccer as

well as the cricket field (both played for Everton and England) put
on 242 in 160 minutes.

Sharp's 150 was reached in under three hours. Once more Hornby
was there when the winning hit was made, this time with five
wickets standing and half an hour to spare. One of the most devastating victories in Lancashire's history was won at Old Trafford,
the victims being Somerset—beaten by an innings and 248 runs
after Lancashire had amassed 558 for 6 scored in under five hours
and illuminated by one of the finest innings in Johnny Tyldesley's
career, 158 runs, many of them from drives of infinite beauty and
power, which brought him 27 fours and enabled him to share with
Alfred Hartley (who scored 234) a partnership reaching 295 in 130
minutes. He was, as usual, especially strong on the off side—though
he would hit the ball all round the wicket with a repertory of strokes
few batsmen have equalled. Slow leg-break bowlers knew desper-
ation when Johnny stepped briskly towards square leg and cut them
to the boundary.

Throughout his cricketing life, which brought him, in first-class
matches more than 37,000 runs including 86 centuries and an
average of over 40, he remained the same quiet, modest and ever-
courteous character he was as a lad from Worsley making his first
diffident appearance at Old Trafford. He was regarded as the perfect
'pro', always 'going', always helpful, especially to younger players,
many of whom owed him a deep debt of gratitude for his advice and
encouragement when he was coach at Old Trafford after his playing
days ended.

This year Fred Reynolds, who had served Lancashire so faith-
fully for forty years as general factotum, steward, collector, assistant
secretary and ground-manager retired—with a good deal of reluctance. There were those who thought that his methods were somewhat out of date and he was often criticised, perhaps unfairly.
A question he was frequently asked by players was—which roller
had he used on the wicket. Almost invariably, whatever was his
answer, he was told that it was the wrong one. Once, in a display of
exasperation, when one of the amateurs said to him: 'Hope it's a
good wicket. Which roller did you put on?' the old man replied:
'All of them.'

It was not easy to find a successor so an advertisement was in-
serted in the newspapers. It read: 'Wanted, a Ground Manager
for County Cricket Ground, Old Trafford. Salary £200 a year,

with house, gas, coal etc.' There were more than three hundred applications from all over the country, those seeking this not very remunerative job including Army and Navy officers, actors and assorted entertainers, including ventriloquists, theatrical managers and others who made no claims to know anything at all about cricket. One of the odder applications came from a man who freely confessed this ignorance but said that he had a brother who kept a pork pie shop near the ground—and gave him as a reference. In the end that fine player of earlier years, R. G. Barlow, was appointed, but he soon found the worries too great and the 'bosses' too numerous and asked to be relieved.

9 *Unpredictable Parkin*

The last four seasons before World War I were rather less productive of imperishable feats than those which had gone before. In 1911 the method of scoring in the championship changed once more, (five points for a win, three for first innings lead). Lancashire were again fourth in 1911 but, in the middle of the season had a wonderful run winning eight games against only one lost and one drawn—three by an innings, two by ten wickets and two by nine wickets.

The next year will always be remembered for the triangular tournaments, damned as a failure though the verdict might have been different if the weather had not been so bad in contrast to warm and sunny 1911. Because of the tournament, county programmes were shortened but the season was not without its highlights. When Surrey visited Old Trafford the two finest batsmen of the day, Reg Spooner and Jack Hobbs, both made centuries and Whitehead achieved the hat-trick. The England-Australia Test at Old Trafford was drawn (like the previous encounter in 1909), Wilfred Rhodes hitting 92 of England's 203, to which Australia replied with 14 for 0 before the rains came. The following season Lancashire would rather forget. It was about the worst in the club's history up to that date. Eleven matches were lost and Lancashire dropped to eighth in the championship. There were relieving features, for instance the astounding joint success of the Tyldesley brothers, Johnny and Ernest in June. Both scored a century against Leicester and followed this record immediately with a repeat performance at the Oval, Johnny hitting 210 and his younger brother 110. In this match of much interest, Hayward completed his hundred hundreds, joining the only other cricketer to achieve this target up to then, W. G. Grace. There were three Roses tussles, an extra fixture being arranged, at Aigburgh, to mark the visit to Liverpool of King George V. Lancashire won two of them.

However the cricketing records, good and bad, were somewhat

overshadowed by controversy over the management of the club. It was started by former captain A. H. Hornby, in a letter to the *Manchester Guardian* in which he criticised a proposal to reduce the number of fixtures and raised various other points. Several reforms resulted, including the introduction of season tickets and the raising of the ban on members taking friends into the pavilion. The financial position was strengthened, too. Lancashire's cricket, however, was still in a depression in 1914, the team sliding further down, to 11th place in the table.

But for the county there was rich promise in the debut of Cecil Parkin, bowler extraordinary and rare 'original', and of Charles Hallows, a left-arm bowler dubbed by his colleagues 'Flight', a nickname which stuck to him through his subsequent fame as a batsman. Parkin had played for Yorkshire at the request of Lord Hawke, though it was against the rigid birth qualification rule as the M.C.C. quickly pointed out. Parkin, born at Egglescliffe, just inside Durham, left Yorkshire after this rebuff and played for Church in the Lancashire League.

He was pleased enough with himself when, in the trial game he was invited to play in at Old Trafford, he took six wickets; and he was bitterly disappointed when he was told that he had not made the grade. It was held that he was not a stayer. He was, at the time, very thin, weighing only nine stone. At 28 he reckoned that his chance of a first-class career had been taken from him a second time. However, he was taking so many wickets in the League that Lancashire decided to try him in the team. After that previous rejection he was reluctant—and the Church Club committee had to persuade him to play. The game was against Leicestershire. Parkin had a match record of 14 wickets for 99 runs. He had 'arrived', and nothing now was said about his stamina.

Parkin, ever an irrepressible character, was conspicuous from the start. One of his victims in that first game for Lancashire was C. J. B. Wood, who had hit two separate hundreds in his previous county match. Parkin, with his spin, had him out for only a few runs and Wood was so annoyed with himself that he knocked all three stumps out of the ground with his bat before retiring. Bowling in a dozen innings that season overshadowed by war clouds, Parkin headed the Lancashire averages, so that *Wisden* commented: 'Had Parkin been available all through the season Lancashire's record might have been far more worthy of the county.' So great an

impression had he made in his first game for the county that, in the
Kent match, Jack Sharp warned Huish, the Kent wicket-keeper:
'Fred, just wait until this lad gets at you; you'll wonder what day
it is.'

Parkin took four wickets. But perhaps the wicket of which Parkin
was proudest was taken at Old Trafford and the victim was that
whirlwind hitter who gave a new adjective to batsmanship, Gilbert
Jessop (the adjective being, need I add, Jessopian). The Gloucestershire captain had, in his carefree way, hit 35 runs in eleven minutes,
including three sixes off the bowling of Harry Dean. Parkin was put
on and the first ball flashed past him to hit the sightscreen with a
resounding whack. The next went into the pavilion enclosure but
the fifth bowled Jessop. As he passed Parkin he said: 'Well bowled,
boy,' a generous word of praise Cecil Parkin never forgot.

As the season progressed and the war drew inexorably nearer,
there was a lack of reality about county cricket and, when fighting
started in Belgium it abruptly ended. Surrey were awarded the
championship and players all over the country packed their cricket
bags, many of them for the last time. The Lancashire players dispersed to various war duties, from which some were not to return.
Parkin was luckier than some; he became a fuel organiser at
Oswaldtwistle and was able to play cricket on Saturdays. Harold
Garnett, Alfred Hartley, W. K. Tyldesley, T. A. Nelson and Egerton
L. Wright were all killed. The Old Trafford pavilion became a
hospital—it was called the Pavilion Hospital—which is was to
remain until February 1919.

Cricket between the wars was a period of prodigal wealth in
personality partnerships. Never in the game's history have there
been so many truly great pairs, batsmen and bowlers, in every
case the two proving to be, as nearly as is possible, the perfect
complement of each other, even if utterly contrasting in style and
temperament—Hobbs and Sutcliffe, Hobbs and Sandham, Holmes
and Sutcliffe, Gregory and McDonald, Gilligan and Tate, Makepeace and Hallows, Woodfull and Ponsford, Hendren and Hearne,
Larwood and Voce, Bowes and Verity...

This same period, when personalities drew the crowds and the
crowds were willing enough to be drawn, was adorned by two of
the greatest all-rounders of all time—surely the greatest England
has produced—Frank Woolley and Wally Hammond. The first

season after the war was, understandably, one of rebuilding, patching up, and earnest searching for new talent. Lancashire were in a more fortunate position than most counties. They had the nucleus of a strong team, though few of its players or supporters could foresee the fame that was to be their's in the 1920s. Many of their younger pre-war players were available, though Cook was not 'demobbed' until late in the season and Parkin, owing to his League committment, was only able to play occasionally. Yet another Tyldesley, James, stepped into the temporarily depleted bowling ranks with his 'quickies to support the hard-working Heap and make up for the evident lack of effectiveness of Dean.

But in batting there was immense strength. Ernest Tyldesley headed the averages, just beating Makepeace and Hallows, clearly now a player of top class. Johnny Tyldesley, though in his 46th year, was often as good as ever he was. For a man of his age his agility and stamina were astonishing, as his 272 against Derbyshire and 170 against Gloucestershire at Old Trafford—including no fewer than 7 sixes and 17 fours—amply proved. That second long score took those who remembered the young J.T. right back to his youthful peak. It was, perhaps, the most aggressive innings of his life and it was played in the company of Ernest, the brothers actually hitting 218 runs in under two hours.

This was the year of the two-days county matches experiment which was not regarded as a resounding success. It had been Lancashire's idea and, like the championship scoring change, it recoiled on them. Twelve of the 24 matches were drawn and, had they run to three days, Lancashire might well have finished higher than fifth in the table. Still, there were some good finishes, none more memorable than the end of the Sussex game at Old Trafford. Lancashire had led on the first innings but Sussex, after Maurice Tate had hit a lusty first century in first-class cricket, set them 273 to win. Sporting Sussex fielded in heavy rain for the last twenty minutes to give their hosts a chance to win—which they did. Hallows, like Tate, had a maiden century.

Spooner came back to lead the side against Surrey, in the absence of the new skipper Myles Kenyon, and a fine bowler made a brief appearance in the team before departing to achieve fame with Kent—C. S. Marriott. Another highly promising Tyldesley, Richard, no relation to J.T. and Ernest, appeared for the first time and, indeed, there were four Tyldesleys in some games, J.T. and

Ernest adding lustre to the batting, Dick and James to the bowling. Dick, unlike James, was a slow bowler. He bowled leg breaks and googlies, but many of his wickets were to come from a ball that did not break at all but gathered vicious momentum off the pitch from top spin. He was bulky and benign, with a full moon face and a drum-like rotundity which fitted well his genial dispostion.

It was sharply realised, when Parkin did play, what a gap was left when he did not. Yorkshire certainly learned this fact of Lancashire life for Parkin took fourteen of their wickets at Old Trafford. Makepeace compiled a solid century and 78, fair enough contributions towards victory by 146 runs with 7 minutes to spare. He was ably supported by James Tyldesley; but it was Parkin's match and he considered afterwards that it was the feat that gave him most joy among so many. As a bowler Parkin, with his bewildering, cunningly devised variations of pace, his spin, his googly and his unflagging gusto, was a match winner on his own.

He was a personality whose every movement compelled attention. The guardsman-like march to his mark, quick turn, duck of his glossy head, the raising of his left arm before the right arm wheeled over with rhythmic grace to release a ball which might be just medium pace or quite devilish fast, can never be forgotten by those who witnessed the wizard's compelling and confounding action—and certainly not by those who strove to combat it. Nor can his conjuring, the flick of the ball from boot to hand, the vanishing ball trick—he could, surely, have made a living 'on the boards', for he was a conjurer up to professional standard.

'Ciss' Parkin will, certainly, be remembered always as a character whose clowning delighted spectators everywhere even if it was not always relished by those in authority. Puckish, unpredictable, he was often hilariously funny, sometimes trying but never negative. He had a habit of singing, usually when his bowling was reaping him rewards, snatches of simple little ditties currently popular. For example, there were occasions when he could be heard, as he ran up to the crease, delivering, 'The sky is blue 'n I love *you*', the *you* emphasized and sometimes accompanying delivery of the ball, which underlined the point by destroying the batsman. Parkin, a bowler of much individuality but undoubted dedication, loved batsmen in the twenties just about as tenderly as did Freddie Trueman in the fifties.

Sir Neville Cardus (in *Cricket all the Year*) tells the story of a typical 'turn', starring Parkin, at Lord's. A misunderstanding with Dick Tyldesley when those renowned bowlers were batting together resulted in them both being at the same end, with Dick still roaring 'Noa'. The ball was thrown in to Parkin's evacuated end and the bowler had only to step forward and remove the bails. Instead he had a shy at the stumps and missed them, the ball racing on to the Nursery. Parkin, reprieved, shouldered arms with his bat and marched with military briskness back to his place—singing as he marched, 'The British Grenadier'.

To be sure Parkin could be a 'problem' for a captain. Sir Pelham ('Plum') Warner said of him that he was 'something of a genius as a bowler but he had too many tricks and too many balls of different types, so that it was not easy to place the field accurately for him.'

Though still playing for Rochdale that first season after the war, Parkin was picked for the Players, captained by J. T. Tyldesley, against the Gentlemen. This entailed his first visit to London. Outside Euston he saw a placard (probably referring to a new item of confectionery) which read: 'Parkin arrives in Town'. Afterwards he confessed that in his innocence he thought to himself: 'How do they know I'm here yet?' He took nine wickets, a milestone on the road to a place in the team for Australia in 1920–21 captained by J. W. H. T. Douglas—when he was still not a full-time county player. In 1920, indeed, Parkin played in only five games for Lancashire, such were the claims of his League club, but he finished at the top of the county's bowling averages.

In the Kent match at Old Trafford for Harry Dean's benefit he took 13 wickets, Kent being dismissed for 104 and 88 in four hours. Though the game was over in two days Dean's benefit was highly satisfactory. In the absence of Parkin, he and Lol Cook often had to bear the brunt of the bowling and a splendid understanding they had. It was exemplified when Hampshire were the visitors at Liverpool. Kennedy had bustled Lancashire out for 57 in the second innings, taking 9 wickets for 33 runs, so that Hampshire wanted only 66 to win. The 'night watchmen', Newman and Evans, got six of them and the proceedings the next day looked to be a formality. There had been more rain and, as Lancashire took the field, Dean said to Cook: 'Don't bowl them out, Lol.' He had astutely assessed that the wicket later might take spin and wanted to keep the tail-enders out there, rather than the regular batsmen, while the pitch was comparatively easy. For one hour they bowled up and down on a length. Then Dean, finding the wicket 'biting', as he had anticipated, said to Cook: 'Now, then, Lol'. The last five wickets fell for ten runs and Lancashire won—by one run. There was a thrilling finish, too, to the race for the championship. Lancashire had looked certain winners just twenty-four hours before the end of the season. They had won their last match and must be champions —unless Middlesex beat Surrey at Lord's. Middlesex were, at that juncture, in a precarious position, Surrey having a substantial first innings lead.

But Middlesex pulled the game out of the fire, setting Surrey a target of 244 and bowling them out 55 runs short of it, with just ten minutes left. The summer of 1921 will always be remembered by those around to enjoy it, for many days of glorious sunshine which turned the playing fields of England brown before it ended, and for the visit of the all-powerful Australian team under the masterful captaincy of Warwick Armstrong. Time had healed some of the scars and dimmed some of the memories of the war, and cricket boomed. Lancashire, in spite of heavy expenditure in restoring and improving the Old Trafford ground, showed a profit of £3,000 and had a membership of 4,661. With a tremendously strong side and fast wickets for their great players to exploit, it was surprising that Lancashire were unable to achieve anything better than fifth place. Ernest Tyldesley and Hallows often dazzled and once more Parkin proved his match-winning capacity. He was still an infrequent member of the team but, against Hampshire at Old Trafford, he took 14 wickets for 180 runs to swing Lancashire to victory from defeat on the stroke of time and by 27 runs, in spite of a first innings deficit and a determined effort by the Hon. Lionel Tennyson, Hampshire's captain, who hit Parkin for 21 in one over. Not that this upset 'Ciss' at all. His answer was to dismiss Hampshire almost on his own, taking 8 wickets in that second innings. Parkin played under Tennyson against the formidable Australians in the Old Trafford match. There were several remarkable features of the game and some amusing interludes.

H. L. ('Herby') Collins of Australia, established a batting 'marathon', staying at the wicket seven hours while he prodded his way to forty runs. As this performance, like Tennyson's brook, seemed to be flowing on for ever, someone in the crowd shouted to the English captain: 'Why don't you read him one of your grand-father's poems?'. Parkin at once replied: 'He has done; that's why he's gone to sleep.' Parkin's next ball had Collins l.b.w.

Parkin's analysis, after bowling all day, proved to be his best in Test cricket, 5 wickets for 33 runs. And what a duel he had had with Herby Collins. What he relished most about that match, however, was the fact that he opened both the bowling and the batting. 'In the whole history of cricket there are only two men who have opened England's bowling and batting against Australia; Wilfred Rhodes was one and I am too modest to tell you the name of the other' he wrote (in *Cricket Triumphs and Troubles*) years later. He explained that what happened was this. Tennyson entered the dressing-room and announced: 'We want some runs quickly'. He told Hallows and J. T. Tyldesley to put their pads on and try to score fast. As a joke (which he never could resist) Ciss Parkin asked: 'What's wrong with me?' The skipper replied: 'You get your pads on and I will follow you.' Parkin thought Tennyson was merely playing up to his quip, then realised that he was serious. Said Parkin as he padded up: 'You won't be required. They will never get me out!'

Parkin duly hit a brisk score of runs, a feat suitably acknow-ledged by the crowd and then, with England 44 for 1 wicket to add to their 362 for 4 declared in the first innings against Australia's unusually modest 175, rain ended the proceedings. E. A. (Ted) McDonald who, with J. M. Gregory formed the fastest attack in the world at the time and were the scourge of the counties all over England, had his first experience of the ground he was to come to love and regard as his own.

Lancashire, in 1922 for the second season in succession, finished fifth in the championship table. For the first half of the summer they had looked to be runaway champions. They won the first seven games but then, unaccountably, declined and lost five of the remain-ing thirteen fixtures, winning only three. Parkin had at least joined them full time. At the end of the previous season Alderman Worsley, a member of the Lancashire Committee, had approached the Rochdale Club and Parkin, saying that his real place was in county cricket. Rochdale then released him.

Jimmy White, the spectacular financier, had been President of Rochdale when Parkin joined them at a record wage of £15 a week and when, some time after he transferred to Lancashire, Parkin met him at a Gentlemen v Players match White said that it was 'ridiculous' that he should have left Rochdale. 'If I had known you were going to leave I would have given you £10,000 to stay' he said—and meant it. Parkin was not so sure that he had done the right thing. However Parkin had by then formed a great affection for Old Trafford 'the best ground in the world—except Sydney and Melbourne—for good light, and for the beautiful greenness of the turf and good wickets', he said, adding that it was always 'matey' and 'the real home of cricket with a happy family atmosphere about it which contributes so much to everyone's enjoyment at all times.' That first full season Cecil Parkin took 172 wickets in the championship at 17 runs each.

The Yorkshire match at Old Trafford in August was a classic example of the dour struggle, neither side giving an inch, which all 'Roses' matches are supposed to be. Certainly it was as tense as any in the series for the two sides between them had the most powerful array of bowlers in the country; for Yorkshire, Robinson, Waddington, Kilner, Macaulay and E. R. Wilson; for Lancashire Parkin, Cook, James Tyldesley and Richard Tyldesley. Considering this phalanx, and a blank Bank Holiday due to rain, a grand total of 500 runs for the loss of 38 wickets was not bad. With five overs to go Yorkshire's last pair were in and five runs were needed. The match was drawn amid tension which must have been felt in Leeds. Was it upon this dramatic occasion that a spectator, applauding, with disgraceful impartiality, both the batting and the fielding side, was challenged by another spectator, who had travelled from Huddersfield. 'Arn't you Lancasheer?' he asked. 'No, I'm not'. 'Then where's t'a from?' 'From London.' 'Well, keep thi' clapper shut. This game's got nowt to do with thee'.

10 *Power and Glory*

Jack Sharp, a native of Hereford who first played for the county in 1899, took over the captaincy from Myles Kenyon. He was one of the outstanding all-round sportsmen of his day. As outside-right for Everton he had played in two Cup Finals and was in the cup winning side at Crystal Palace. He had also been capped for England. As a cricketer he was in Lancashire's championship winning side in 1904 and played for England against Australia in 1909. At the Oval, though he had been selected as a fast bowler, he hit the only century achieved by an England player in that series. He was a hard-hitting batsman and fine cover point. In a long career—26 years—he scored more than 20,000 runs and took 448 wickets, which places him high indeed among Lancashire's all-rounders. He proved a good captain too and, under him, the county finished third, fourth and then third again.

Those were years of Yorkshire domination before the red rose ousted the white, but in Sharp's last season he had the satisfaction of leading his side to victory in 19 of the 32 championship games. Parkin and Dick Tyldesley had to bowl and bowl in 1923, for Cook's form had virtually deserted him and James Tyldesley's death had been a severe blow to the team of which he was not only a valuable but a popular member. So it was that the new captain was without a fast bowler, his own fast bowling days being over. Though R. Tyldesley took more than 100 wickets it was largely Parkin's season, for he had 176 in championship matches, 209 altogether.

The batting was very strong, Makepeace joining J.T. and Ernest Tyldesley, the only Lancashire batsmen hitherto to top 2,000 runs in a season. But the events of greater significance for the county's future were the qualification, by residence, of Ted McDonald, who had decided to settle here and play county, rather than league cricket, and the debut of George Duckworth, of Warrington, a great wicket-keeper and one of the game's imperishable characters. No

Lancashire player has been so abundantly Lancashire, no stumper has been more nimble and certainly none more vocal. Duckworth's appeals became a feature of cricket at Old Trafford and all other cricket grounds upon which he appeared. It was not so much an appeal as an assertion. He was directing the umpire in his bounden duty and he wanted his decision to be known far beyond the boundaries of Stretford, to say nothing of echoing up and down the Warwick Road line. If he were appealing for l.b.w., then the 'Howzat?' which was at once a yell of triumph and of execration, would be supplemented by an uplifted finger.

Umpires being, necessarily, a tough breed, many of these verbal-cum-mime dismissals were overruled. But many were not. For Lancashire in 424 matches Duckworth caught 634 batsmen and stumped 287 more of them. In one season, 1928, his bag was 107, an astonishing total. No county had a combination so aggressive, so menacing as George Duckworth and Ted McDonald, the best fast bowler of his day and, some say, of any day. Time and again would Duckworth, crouching low, leap cat-like to his left to pounce, with chilling shriek, upon the suspected deflection.

No wicket-keeper had quite such variety to deal with as had Duckworth with the fiery McDonald, the unpredictable Parkin, always dreaming up a new ball and always altering pace, and Dick Tyldesley with his 'proper diddles' and perspiring persistence. It was fitting that Lancashire, in its Diamond Jubilee year, should have one of the best sides in its history. To say that 'they was robbed' is to understate the dolorous position. Every home fixture except one, at Blackpool, suffered some interruption from the vile weather and only two out of twelve Old Trafford games were finished. For McDonald it was a season of some frustration, for Parkin one of triumph—and tragedy. Parkin took 200 wickets once more and came third in the national averages behind only Macaulay and Kilner from across the border, but some indiscreet views published under his name ended his Test career. He was accused of criticising Arthur Gilligan's captaincy in the Test match against South Africa at Birmingham—the celebrated occasion when Gilligan and Tate bowled the tourists out for 30.

Parkin explained later that the article, which appeared in a Sunday paper, had been written by a journalist friend he had asked to oblige him by 'putting a few lines together and wiring them' for him and that he did not know the contents. He denied that he had ever criticised Gilligan for not putting him on or for anything else, and he wrote to England's captain apologising for the article's appearance. Gilligan accepted gracefully and said that he regarded the incident as closed. So far as Parkin was concerned, however, the damage was irreparable and the Birmingham test proved to be his last.

There was a touch of irony, perhaps, in the fact that two of Parkin's best feats were against Gilligan's Sussex—13 wickets at Hove and 10 at Old Trafford. McDonald, on his first appearance for the county, had 5 Kent wickets and he, Parkin and Dick Tyldesley captured 366 inexpensive championship wickets between them. The most remarkable bowling feat—and game, come to that —was shared by Parkin and Tyldesley. Lancashire were routed for 49 by Glamorgan, a débâcle so surprising that telegrams, anticipating victory, were sent to the Glamorgan captain, J. C. Clay and his bowlers, from a number of South Welsh fans. While they were being opened Glamorgan were demolished in their turn—for 22. Makepeace and Hallows, who shared so many fine opening partnerships, scored sufficient runs to ensure victory for their side.

For McDonald, 1925 was a tremendous year which brought him 205 wickets; Tyldesley had 116 and Parkin 121. But at the top of the county averages was a new name soon to become familiar, Frank Sibbles. His 43 wickets that first season cost only 13 runs each. With such a talented team it was not surprising that gates were big. Even at Nelson, given a fixture as part of the deal to release McDonald from the League club to the county, there was an attendance exceeding 10,000. And a huge crowd for the last game of the season, at Old Trafford, saw a new record stand against them on that ground, 330 by Hammond (250) and and Dipper (144).

This was the occasion of Jack Sharp's farewell, and his 75 in 2½ hours, though on the slow side, brought him a big ovation. Leonard Green now took over the captaincy and few skippers have ever had such a triumphant run of successes. For three years Lancashire reigned as champions, in the third year by a margin so wide that no-one could dispute their right to regard themselves as the team of the decade. Green had the gift of leadership clearly necessary to maintain authority over a team of stars. McDonald was now recognised as the finest fast bowler in the country, perhaps in the world. He was most ably supported by Sibbles, Parkin and Richard Tyldesley.

Sibbles had the distinction of twice taking the wicket of Jack Hobbs at Old Trafford, a valuable contribution to a Lancashire victory by 34 runs, in the last over. But the man who saved the day, and many another day that summer which started with a massive interruption, not by rain but by the general strike, was Ernest Tyldesley. His fighting innings after Surrey had led by 95 runs, turned the tide. Tyldesley, who never had the full recognition he so richly deserved, in one month from the end of June scored 1,128 runs in nine innings and hit seven centuries in consecutive matches, an astonishing run. In the Old Trafford Test match against Australia, one of many abortive because of rain, he hit a sound 81 towards England's 305 for 5 in reply to Australia's massive 494, made up mainly of Woodfull's 141, a majestic 151 by C. G. ('the Guv'nor General') Macartney, and A. J. Richardson's 109.

Ernest Tyldesley, indeed, had one success after another. He actually hit a half century or more in ten consecutive innings, a feat only equalled by Sir Donald Bradman. Here are his scores between June 26th and August 6th—144, 69 and 144 not out, 226 (v Sussex at Old Trafford), 51 and 131, 131 again (for the Players at Lord's), 106, 126, 81, 44, 139 (v Yorkshire at Old Trafford), and 85.

That last score was made against Middlesex at Old Trafford, a game remembered chiefly for the fact that McDonald scored his only century in first-class cricket. Lancashire did not win the championship without a mighty struggle. Yorkshire, champions for four seasons, were in the lead until Lancashire, all guns blazing —and this was a team of big guns—destroyed Northants and then Notts. The match with the latter, last of the season, clinched the matter, and at Old Trafford, too. Exultant supporters revelled in the express bowling of McDonald, who took eleven wickets, and a tremendous stand by Makepeace and Ernest Tyldesley—279 out of 454. Tyldesley's record at the end of that memorable season, was so astonishingly similar to that of his brother, J. T., 22 years before that it is worth setting out:

		Inns.	N.O.	Highest	Runs	Av.
1904	J. T. Tyldesley	37	5	225	2,237	69·90
1926	E. Tyldesley	38	4	226	2,365	69·55

Tyldesley was a batsman of great resource. He could be a 'grafter' as the Australians put it; he could also produce a dazzling range of strokes, and he could hit the ball very hard indeed—as he did against Somerset during that summer he made his own. G. F. Earle, who was almost in the Jessop bracket among batsmen, had put the ball through a window in the Taunton pavilion. Tyldesley, in the course of his now almost inevitable century, hit a six—through the same window. Such a hefty straight drive was more characteristic of the Somerset amateur than the Lancashire professional, in fact.

Parkin had a vivid memory of a Somerset match at Old Trafford. Earle hit a ball from him so hard that, in his own words, it 'travelled nearly two fields away, almost to Ted McDonald's house at the Old Trafford end of the ground'. The next morning Parkin went to 'Mr' Earle (amateurs were never without the prefix in those days) and said: 'Mr Earle, you owe me 4/6d.' 'Whatever for, Parkin?' the Somerset batsman enquired. 'For the taxi I paid for to go and fetch that ball you hit yesterday,' the ill-used bowler replied. The saddest episode of Tyldesley's summer was the dropping of Parkin and his departure from county cricket. He had failed to exploit a wicket which formerly would have been regarded as made for him and the Committee decided that he was on the decline. After his omission from the team Parkin resigned and his resignation was accepted. His fans, who thought that he should not have been allowed to leave, pointed to the fact that he had, up to then, taken 39 wickets at only 16 runs apiece. But the decision was irrevocable.

Parkin, the whimsical comic, could be and sometimes was melodramatic. He had told the Committee that he felt that he was no longer wanted and that he was leaving with something 'no one in the world could purchase—a good character'. Holding out his hands he declared: 'God has given me these hands to work with, and I will carry on with them even if I have to be a tramp.' This proved unnecessary—the hands, or one of them, reaped him many more wickets in the next eleven years and until he was well over fifty. Parkin did not bear resentment and his affection for Old Trafford remained deep to the end of his life. Indeed, his ashes were scattered on the Old Trafford pitch as he had wished—and that delightfully evocative writer, the late A. A. Thomson, describing this melancholy ceremony, used a phrase which would surely have delighted Parkin himself: 'You can almost hear a ghostly voice murmur, "Scatter me at the Stretford end, lads; I could always find a good spot from there . . ." '

And Parkin's 'greats', in his latter years, were Lancashire
players. Who else? The greatest bowler of all time, he asserted,
was Barnes, who was so correct that it was 'impossible for him to
bowl bad balls', and the greatest fast bowler was Ted McDonald.
Of him Parkin said with awe: 'He could keep on bowling for a
couple of hours yet there was not a bead of perspiration on his
forehead.' McDonald had a reputation for dourness but Parkin
insisted that he had a quaint dry humour of his own. Dry, and perhaps pawky. He would say to a bowler who had dropped a catch
off his bowling, 'Never mind, you'll catch one some time'. But he
never complained and, though he thought Armstrong the greatest
captain of all, his devotion to Lancashire was complete.

McDonald was the spearhead of the powerful Lancashire bowling
in 1927, but so wet was that summer—only 110 out of a total of
240 championship fixtures were finished—that on a number of
occasions he reduced his great pace to bowl spinners. He was,
according to Sir Neville Cardus, 'prouder of his medium-paced
off-breaks from round the wicket than of his pace', a predilection
which had proved very nearly disastrous on a hard wicket with
Woolley and Hardinge batting for Kent during the season before.
Lancashire lost only one match but the team had to put up with a
good deal of criticism of its slow batting—which almost lost them
the championship. Indeed, when Gloucestershire visited Old
Trafford in mid-season Lancashire looked to be trailing, especially
when Wally Hammond, against McDonald, not indulging his
spinning fancy but bowling at his fastest, hit one of the most magnificent innings ever seen on that ground, 187 at a run a minute, the
ball sizzling to all points of the compass.

This drawn game, however, was followed by five victories taking
Lancashire back to the top. This spell of success included a resounding victory over Yorkshire at Old Trafford, McDonald taking
eleven wickets. Jack Iddon, from Mawdesley, near Ormskirk, 25-
years-old son of a professional cricketer, now emerged as a fine
all-rounder. It could be said that his left hand spin bowling was a
significant factor in Lancashire's recovery. Against Warwickshire
at Old Trafford he took three cheap wickets in the first innings and
6 for 22 in the second, shooting the Midlanders out for 64 and
turning an almost certain draw into an inspiring victory.

Against Surrey he hit his first century in an innings which
reached 522 for 9. This match produced a classic duel between

McDonald and D. R. Jardine, who scored a century and stimulated *Wisden* to this prophetic (when one remembers the 'body-line' rumpus five years later) comment: 'Jardine faced the bumping bowling of McDonald with rare skill'. As the season progressed it became clear that Notts were Lancashire's rivals for the championship, and the match at Trent Bridge was followed all over the country as keenly as if it were a Test. Lancashire's fielding was far from what it had been in previous years so that Notts piled up 420 runs and, after Sam Staples had disposed of the visitors for a puny 148, the championship looked like changing hands. However Lancashire batsmen could be dour—and dour, at this critical juncture, they were. Hallows, emulating Barlow at his Bailey-like Barnacle best, stayed at the wicket for more than two hours for seven runs. Then the rain came. Lancashire next lost to Sussex and yielded the lead once more to Notts. Their last match was drawn and they had to await, with as much composure as they could contrive, the outcome of Nottinghamshire's encounter with Glamorgan to know their fate. Notts were favourites for a win and the title. Then a miracle, or a catastrophe, depending upon which side you favoured, was wrought. Mercer and Ryan bowled out Notts for 61 and Lancashire retained the championship by less than 1 per cent. There were no such last minute doubts and changes of fortune the following year, however.

Lancashire were unquestionably the greatest team in the championship, going through their programme without a single defeat. Prolific were the run getters and none more so than Hallows. He achieved the rare feat of scoring 1,000 runs in May, thus: 100, 101 and 51 not out, 22, 74 and 104, 58 and 34 not out, 232 (v. Sussex at Old Trafford). In his benefit match he made a modest 36 but the scoring was terrific—1,155 runs for the loss of only 13 wickets, Sandham hit 282 of Surrey's 567 before retiring ill and Watson broke Lancashire's individual score record, 295 by J. T. Tyldesley in 1902, with 300 not out. His stand of 371 with Ernest Tyldesley set up another record and took Lancashire into the lead with 588 for 4 wickets.

Watson and Hallows put on more than a hundred runs for the first wicket twelve times that unforgettable season. Watson, Hallows and Tyldesley all topped 2,000 runs in championship matches and Tyldesley's triumphs included 160 not out in a Test trial and 122 against the West Indies, both at Lord's. The colossal batting power of the trio was seen at its most impressive when Kent visited Old Trafford. Woolley was at his brilliant best and Kent were 262 for 4 when McDonald and Sibbles struck. The last six Kent men (or men of Kent, or both) were dismissed for 15 runs. Watson and Hallows then opened with 155, Hallows and Ernest Tyldesley proceeding to add 207 before the captain declared. McDonald then bowled unchanged, emerging with a match analysis of 15 for 154, and Kent's second innings reached no more than 113.

In a year of such batting dominance McDonald had a remarkably fine record—178 wickets at 19 runs each. The next best bowler was Dick Tyldesley with 85 at just under 31 apiece. The West Indians, in spite of some dazzling performances by Learie Constantine (now Lord Constantine) were no match for England who won all three Tests, at Old Trafford by an innings and 30 (compared with an innings and 58 at Lord's and an innings and 71 at the Oval).

The years after Lancashire's triple triumph saw many changes. P. T. Eckersley, who had played some useful rather than spectacular innings, was now captain and it was evident that a period of remoulding faced the new skipper. McDonald was not likely to continue to be the force he had been so long—there is a limit to the number of peak years for any fast bowler—and the same applied to Makepeace who, in 1929 was in his 47th year. But quite unexpected blows fell in a loss of form by Hallows which cost him his place in the team, and the decision of Richard Tyldesley to leave the county following a pay dispute. Though McDonald and Makepeace were nearing the end of their lustrous careers, both contributed handsomely to Lancashire's modified success, tie-ing for second place behind Nottinghamshire, the new champions. McDonald took 140 wickets (followed by Dick Tyldesley with 136, the next highest tally being 44) and Makepeace headed the batting averages. The team's first defeat since August 1927 (when the Rev. F. B. R. Browne, known as 'Tishy' on account of a weird 'whirligig' action, and Tate bowled them out for 99 and 76, and Skipper Gilligan hit a century towards an innings win) was inflicted, again, by Sussex, K. S. Duleepsinhji scoring a superb hundred.

Overshadowing the return of Lancashire to the top and the stirring doings of its batsmen in the summer of 1930 was the remarkable record of a young man named Donald George Bradman, aged twenty-one, from New South Wales, Australia. In spite of the cold wet weather that summer he scored nearly 3,000 runs averaging more than 98 and wrote himself into the history books (as well as paving the way to the unprecedented tribute of Yorkshire Honorary Membership) with his record 334 against England at Headingley in one day and twenty minutes. The Old Trafford Test, a rain-enforced draw, brought him no success and his recollections of Manchester were rather less glowing than those associated with Leeds. Lancashire, indeed, failed to live up to its reputation for hospitality so far as his appearances upon the cricket field were concerned. At Liverpool the policy of setting an Aussie to bowl an Aussie paid off—McDonald 'castle-d' the new young star. Richard Tyldesley had the odd experience of missing his own benefit match because he was playing for England at Trent Bridge. The England captain, A. P. F. Chapman and the rest of the Test team sent an appeal to the Lancashire crowd not to allow his absence to affect the fund. The response was generous.

11 *'Old Shake'—Exemplar*

Makepeace had made his last appearance and McDonald's decline in 1931 was so rapid that he took part in only 14 matches—taking 26 wickets costing 39 runs each—and his contract was terminated by mutual consent. He returned to League cricket. Watson had a prolonged illness and Hallows failed to find his form so that Lancashire were a good deal weaker than they had been or had expected to be. The solidarity of Harry Makepeace was much missed. 'Old Shake' as he was known among the pros, had been a bit of a stickler for what he believed in, a tough senior pro who took cricket seriously and expected others, especially his juniors, to do likewise. He was a fine batsman but he did not dazzle in the MacLaren-Spooner-Tyldesley tradition. As batsman and, later, as coach, he displayed and abjured caution. It was said that his dictum was 'No fours before lunch'. At any rate he was very critical of any careless or reckless hitting out—as many a young player knew to his cost, and perhaps to his lasting benefit.

When Lancashire played Yorkshire at Sheffield, a young batsman of promise joined 'Old Shake' at the wicket and, in the last over but one before the lunch interval hit George Macaulay for two fours. Makepeace strode down the pitch and 'had a word' with the venturesome young swashbuckler. Afterwards this batsman revealed that Mr Makepeace had 'carried on awful'. Not that 'Old Shake' was a slouch in the matter of scoring. Between 1906 and 1930 he hit 25,000 runs, including 43 centuries, one against Australia.

Like other grand cricketers he had his mannerisms. One was to remove his cap and go out to pat down the turf (or 'do a bit of gardening' as the commentators are prone to say) but not before he was really set. When this was observed someone on the players' balcony would inevitably prophesy: 'Old Shake will get a hundred today'. And often enough he did. Ernest Tyldesley also removed his cap when a century looked likely, handing it over to the umpire to complete his innings bareheaded. Harry Makepeace, whatever his harmless little idiosyncracies, belonged to Old Trafford just as much as the Hornbys and Barlow, Briggs and old Reynolds. He spent much of his life there and loved every square inch of it.

In his latter years he was coach and he commanded the deepest respect not only because of his vast knowledge of the game and his facility to impart it but for his own heroic (especially in the eyes of the youngsters undergoing trials) sporting background. He was a double international, in soccer as well as cricket, and possessed both a cup-winner's medal (Everton 1905–6) and a League championship medal (Everton 1913–14). Brian Statham, as a young unknown, regarded him with awe which was soon accompanied by real affection. Playing against Royston he had bowled Jock Livingstone, the Australian who had captained the Commonwealth team which toured India in 1949–50 and had settled here. Livingstone drove without delay to Old Trafford to tell Harry Makepeace he thought he had seen a man to succeed Dick Pollard.

Makepeace greeted Statham before his trial with: 'I have been here a long time, lad, and it has been a happy time. Come, let's see what you can do.' But the old disciplinarian was still there. When Statham, in a trial game, bowled Bob Berry with an off-spinner, instead of receiving the expected approbation from Makepeace he was told sternly: 'You're on trial as a fast bowler so bowl quick.' Nevertheless Statham, like many other Lancashire cricketers, acknowledged a deep debt of gratitude to 'Old Shake' for his advice and encouragement.

There was an altogether new look about the Lancashire team in 1932. Ernest Tyldesley was now the sole remaining member of either family bearing that name, carrying on a tradition going back to 1895. He was again the most successful batsman but another Lancashire and England star was rising, Eddie Paynter, and Iddon confirmed his claim to be one of the best all-rounders in the country. Paynter, short, alert, fluent left hand batsman and superb cover-point had spent a lot of time on the ground staff, 'knocking at the door' but unable to gain entrance because of the side's great batting strength. In fact he might have left the staff but for the faith and encouragement of T. A. (Tommy) Higson, the Honorary Treasurer, who had played for the county in earlier years. The failing form of Charles Hallows gave him his chance. But he was thirty when two elegant centuries in 1931 drew attention to his potential, underlined by a truly great 152 against Yorkshire at Bradford in 1932. It was one of the most thrilling displays of beautifully aggressive batting in all Roses matches and Yorkshire as always, were a formidable bowling side. On a wicket by no means easy Paynter decided that attack was the best method of defence. He hit five sixes, four of them off Hedley Verity, two into the stand and two over the stand into the football ground—prodigious hits. When Leyland replaced Verity he magnanimously offered Paynter a pint for every six he hit off him. The six with which he did earn his beer was a glorious hook high over square leg. It was altogether a remarkable game. Yorkshire, after the pitch had been artificially dried, were spun out by Sibbles and Hopwood for 46. Sibbles, with his off-breaks and accuracy, took 7 wickets for 10 runs, following this up with 5 for 58, and Lancashire won by an innings and 50.

Paynter had shown his capacity for sticking it out, in contrast with the dazzling pyrotechnics of which he was equally capable, in the Roses match the year before, saving the game with a determined 45 not out and then, without removing his pads, 87 not out in the follow-on. But it was that towering Bradford innings which set him on the road to Test fame, achieved on his first tour with Douglas Jardine's controversy-gathering team in Australia; there he turned the game at Adelaide with an admirable 77 and ensured immortality at Brisbane by leaving a hospital bed to play an heroic innings of 83 which, very properly, ended with a six to win the game and the rubber. Paynter could be dour or devastatingly punishing—as he was when he made his highest score, 322 (only beaten in Lancashire's records by MacLaren's 424) at Hove in five hours, the first hundred before lunch.

Eddie, as the then well-populated world of cricket followers knew him, Teddy to his team mates, was a gay and tremendously zestful character. He was a very fine outfield as well as cover, running with rare speed—as he did between the wickets—and equipped with a tremendous throw-in. He was vastly entertaining and (as A. W. Ledbrooke recalls in *Lancashire County Cricket 1864–1953*) he would keep the team happy even while waiting for a connection at Crewe station after midnight, by turning cartwheels or telling stories.

Lancashire, always willing to innovate, took part in the experiment of keeping play going until 8 p.m. if there was a chance of finishing a game on the second day. But there was no enthusiasm for the idea and it was dropped. Iddon figured in a county record at Old Trafford, he and H. R. W. Butterworth hitting 278 for the 6th wicket. Iddon's share was 200, short by only 22 of his career best. Eckersley, a popular captain, insisted on keen fielding and, with Duckworth to help him set an example, the standard rose markedly. The following season, almost as fine as 1921, brought a crop of new players with bright futures to the side—Washbrook and Pollard, who were to play for England, Phillipson, who was unlucky not to do so, and W. H. Lister, the future Lancashire captain and, in later years, President.

Washbrook and Phillipson both played their first games for Lancashire against Sussex at Old Trafford—and Phillipson made his mark, not as the fine bowler he was to become, but as a batsman.

After Sussex had captured 9 wickets for 209, Phillipson and P. T. Eckersley put on 102 runs for the last wicket. Eighteen years old Cyril Washbrook was off the mark from the start, from a career point of view, with a useful score in the second innings, and he established himself as a real find in the next match, against Surrey, hitting 152—by an odd coincidence exactly repeating the feat of J. T. Tyldesley in his second match for the county 38 years earlier. The Yorkshire game at Old Trafford once more evoked criticism of the pitch. It was described as villainous and, unfortunately for Lancashire, the depth of its villainy was reserved for them. Yorkshire, after losing their big guns, Holmes, Sutcliffe and Leyland fairly early, stuck it out until the morning of Whit Monday, by which time, with 341 to their credit, the pitch was becoming not only evil but dangerous. George Macaulay, with his fast off-breaks lifting viciously, took 7 wickets for 28 in Lancashire's first innings and 5 for 21 in the follow on, an innings distinguished by a last wicket stand between Paynter and a South African fast bowler, Gordon Hodgson, who was said to have shut his eyes and clouted 'em. This was Lancashire's only defeat of the season, yet they were no higher than fifth, a situation rectified the following summer when the championship was regained. This was a young team—average age 28—but a number of the younger players had by now useful experience and the benefit of the side's veteran, Ernest Tyldesley, aged 35, as their exemplar.

There were no real pace bowlers but the fielding was now of a high standard and the eleven included an exceptional number of all-rounders. A minor factor (but a morale booster) was Eckersley's luck with the toss. In thirty championship matches Lancashire batted first 24 times—so effectively that there were 18 declarations and 13 victories, more than any other county. The most dramatic event of the season was a clash between Lancashire and their old opponents, often rivals for the title, Nottinghamshire. The 'bodyline' (or 'leg-theory', depending on your allegiance) controversy still followed Larwood and Voce—and Lancashire were officially against this heat-engendering method of attack. There was, indeed, fierce argument in one of the dressing rooms before the start of the match against Notts. at Trent Bridge. Larwood, no doubt goaded by the renewed rumpus, bowled as fast as ever he did in his life. Those who were present declared it to be the most brilliant exhibition of real speed bowling they had ever seen. In spite of catches dropped by the five slip fielders, Lol Larwood had, at one stage, taken 6 wickets for one run. Lancashire were all out for 119 and, when Larwood's turn to bat came, he treated his critics with fine contempt, hitting 80 in 45 minutes including 6 sixes and 8 fours. Notts. reached 266 and looked certain winners. But Lancashire now staged one of the most spectacular and courageous recoveries in all their history.

Against the tremendously fast attack of Larwood and Voce, bumpers and all, Tyldesley hit one of the finest of all his 102 centuries in big cricket. With the aid of split second timing and sheer guts, Tyldesley hooked both Larwood and Voce time and again, so that Eckersley, who had contributed a valuable 40 following 63 by Watson and 86 by Lister, was able to declare at 394 for 7 wickets. A draw looked almost certain; a win was just a dream. But now the slow bowlers took charge. Hopwood, backed up by Iddon's immaculate length, took six wickets and a wholly dramatic match had a breath-taking climax. With the last Notts. man at the wicket, Hopwood and Duckworth—or Hopwood drowned by Duckworth—appealed as they had several times before and this time the umpire's as well as Duckworth's finger went up. An 'impossible' match had been won, by 101 runs. The Lancashire players were exultant. There were impromptu jigs and stumps were thrown in the air. The sequel was more depressing—like the distant rantings of a tedious new figure on the German political scene named Adolf Hitler.

Lancashire batsmen complained to their committee of the battering they had suffered from the Notts. fast bowlers. As a result no fixtures were made with Notts. the following season, though the rift was healed the year after. Ernest Tyldesley passed two milestones, taking him into the highest realm of batsmanship—his hundredth hundred and a new individual record aggregate, beating his brother's 32,267 career runs. The Test match at Old Trafford was so high scoring as to be inevitably inconclusive. England amassed 627 for 9 wickets (Patsy Hendren contributing 132 and Maurice Leyland 153) and 123 for 0. Australia replied with 491 and 66 for 1.

Duckworth added to his many achievements, conceding not a single bye in a Middlesex innings of 465.

The 1935 season was not outstanding in Lancashire's annals, the county falling to fourth place and losing six matches compared with twelve won. But they won a spectacular game at Dover after Kent had built up a lead of 165 in the first innings. Lancashire faced the daunting task of scoring 396 runs in five hours. Watson and Hopwood knocked off the first 103 runs in 90 minutes, Hopwood and Iddon hit 149 in 105 minutes and Paynter and Tyldesley carried on the relay race to give their side victory with 18 minutes left. Tyldesley and Iddon missed a number of games through illness but the arrival of Norman (Buddy) Oldfield strengthened the much weakened batting. In the November General Election that year P. T. Eckersley was elected MP for the Exchange Division of Manchester and the two candidates for the Lancashire captaincy put forward to succeed him were the amateur, W. H. L. Lister and the 46 years old Ernest Tyldesley who had, on a number of occasions captained the side in the absence of the regular skipper —as his elder brother had before him. The diehards still regarded it as essential that the captain of a county side should be an amateur and Lister was elected on a 13-6 vote by the committee. Ernest Tyldesley played a couple of times as an amateur, scoring 34 and 12 not out against Yorkshire at Leeds and 22 against Surrey in Jack Iddon's benefit match at Old Trafford, and then retired. It was the end of an epoch spanning more than forty years during which time there had always been a Tyldesley playing for Lancashire.

Though Ernest was not a flambuoyant character he was, at the crease, without a doubt a classic batsman of confidence and composure. He had the consummate skill and the artistry to make even the best bowling look mediocre. And so unostentatious was he that it was difficult to realise what a truly impressive record he had maintained—an average of 45 over twenty-seven years, which was five runs an innings higher than his illustrious brother achieved.

In 1936 Lancashire suffered the worst season since 1914, falling to 11th among the counties, a record only ameliorated by a late flowering in August when Eddie Paynter hit three memorable centuries in successive innings and his side won five matches. He and Iddon (who hit five centuries) brought some joy to the faithful at Old Trafford with a joint score of 182 in under two hours against Glamorgan, the visitors further obliging by yielding to Dick Pollard 8 wickets for 42 runs. This apart, the most remarkable match at Old Trafford was the Test between England and India which was drawn. Nothing very remarkable about that result at Manchester, to be sure but on one day, July 27th, the total number of runs scored was—588. India had scored a modest 203 in their first innings the day before and England had started to run up a long score. Upon that memorable second day England added 398 runs to bring their total to 571 (Hammond having contributed 167 of them, the first hundred in as many minutes) and, at the close, India's second innings had yielded 190 runs without loss.

India, thereafter, proceeded to 390 for 5, V. M. Merchant hitting 114 and Mustaq Ali 112, so that the considerable Old Trafford crowds could not complain that they had been denied an exhibition of batsmanship. And, to facilitate their journey to the ground, the M.S.J. and A. Railway, proclaiming its electric service of fast and frequent trains to and from Warwick Road station, announced special single fares from the very heart of Manchester, 2d. from Oxford Road and 3d. from London Road. Moreover, leading Regimental Club and Old Boy ties always in stock, could be obtained for 2s. 9d. and blazers to measure for 18s. 6d. Those were the days.

The imagination boggles, in the light of post-war performances, at the remarkable fact that Cyril Washbrook, then 23 and in his fifth year of first class cricket, was dropped from the Lancashire team in 1937. He returned, however, to demonstrate how wrong this rustication had been, hitting three centuries in four innings and establishing himself as opener with Paynter. As the season advanced they put on 268 together upon the occasion when Paynter made hs triple century. With Oldfield, Paynter added another 277. His was the highest innings ever played by a Lancashire professional and an indelible example of sustained power. Iddon was

held largely responsible for a meritorious win over Yorkshire despite a hundred by the champion of all Roses batsmen (he made
more than 3,000 runs against Lancashire) Herbert Sutcliffe. Oldfield assisted with a polished half century.

Following this satisfactory outcome, Lancashire had the morti-
fication of losing both Yorkshire matches in 1938 though they
ascended to a more respectable rung on the county ladder, the
fourth compared with 9th and 11th in the preceeding seasons.
Duckworth, in his 37th year, retired, to be succeeded by Farrimond,
who had on occasion deputised for him and was good enough to be
number one in any team without a stumper of Duckworth's calibre
—which meant any team but Lancashire. Frank Sibbles, too, had
come to the end of his career—untimely, at 34—due to an arm
injury. In twelve seasons he had taken 932 wickets at an average
cost of 22·11 runs.

Among the older hands remaining Paynter was outstanding, and
only Hammond in England that year scored more runs. Against
Australia at Trent Bridge Paynter was top scorer with 216 not out,
a glorious innings which overshadowed even Hutton's 100, Bar-
nett's 126 and Denis Compton's 102. England reached the huge
total of 658 for 8 (other centurions in an inevitably drawn match
yielding 1,069 runs for only 18 wickets being S. J. McCabe, 232,
W. A. Brown, 133 and D. G. Bradman, 144 not out). At Old
Trafford, alas!, 'persistent rain prevented play'. Not a ball was
bowled and, in fact, the captains did not toss up and no final
choice of teams was even announced.

Rain was also a dismal factor of the 1939 programme, ended
abruptly by the onset of the second world war. From mid-July to
August 4th was a period of such deep depression, climatically as
well as politically, that there was not even a first innings decision,
let alone a result.

Still, that summer, with the war clouds gathering ever more
menacingly, with Hitler's consumption of carpet ever increasing
and his shouts for lebensraum ever shriller, was not without its
pleasanter cricketing recollections. Iddon had a splendid season all
round, Washbrook scored more than 1,500 runs though he failed
to get a century, and little Oldfield rejoiced the hearts of all good
Lancastrians by earning an England cap, playing against the West
Indies at the Oval. The weather, as it has so often, ruined the Old
Trafford Test which was left drawn after England, in a vain attempt

to beat the tourists and the weather, had declared twice. The season ended very abruptly at Old Trafford. The Oval having been taken over, Surrey had gone up there for the second time. Pollard, in great form, having recently achieved a hat-trick against Glamorgan, took ten wickets. And then, on the third day September 1st, 1939, anticipating Premier Chamberlain's announcement two days later the game was abandoned and the players dispersed to their various wartime tasks. The Old Trafford ground, buildings and all, was requisitioned by the Army, and the Royal Engineers moved in. After Dunkirk the ground became a transit camp for the evacuated troops on their way to new stations or home. The stands, steps, virtually every spot where a man could lay his weary head, became one vast dormitory, and providentially—the weather remained fine.

12 *Rebuilding*

Lancashire faced a more formidable team-building task than any other county for the first season after the war. Only four of the pre-war side were available as the dependable base upon which to build it: Washbrook, Place, Phillipson and Pollard. Jack Iddon had been killed in a road accident the day after the pre-season lunch at the ground, Hopwood had retired, Eddie Paynter, Buddy Oldfield (who later went to Northamptonshire), stumper Farrimond, Reg Parkin and Nutter had all left county cricket for the Leagues and, on top of all this, Wilkinson, who had shown promise as a slow-bowler, injured a leg in the first match and never recovered his pre-war form. The team even lost its captain before the programme started, T. A. Higson Jun. finding business pressures too great to take it on.

J. A. Fallows, son of the Lancashire C.C.C.'s honorary treasurer, stepped into the vacant boots and great credit he earned not only for moulding a team with little material to start with, but for imperturbably facing much hostility. For the choice of Fallows had been severely criticised, to put it mildly. He was 39, he had a puny Minor Counties average, the highest score of his cricketing life had been a century for Manchester many years before and he had spent the previous six years in the Army. This last factor was in his favour with the Committee. He had risen from the ranks to Lt. Colonel and clearly commanded the loyalty of the men under him. And, if his enthusiasm for the game out-galloped his skill, at least it was burning, unquenchable.

Once more it was proved that the opportunity makes the man. Fallows, genial but forthright and astute, wrought that almost new side into a fine, integrated, aggressive combination to challenge the leaders and finish a season which had such dismal auspices third in the championship table with 200 points compared with Yorkshire's 216 and Middlesex's 204. Somerset, fourth, were way behind with 166 points. In the circumstances it was a remarkable achievement and nobody worried about the fact that Fallows was bottom of the batting averages with 8·14 (Washbrook was at the top with 71·77). Only a year before it had looked as if Lancashire would not only be without a captain and a team, but a ground. One dark morning in December 1940 Old Trafford had been blitzed. As a veteran member recalled: 'The hearts of many of us were heavy as we surveyed the damage done by the enemy bombers. We doubted if cricket would ever again be played at Old Trafford. All but one stand on the popular side, had suffered greatly. There was a mound of earth in what had once been a green carpet of outfield. As if by a miracle, the hallowed "middle" was unscarred, the wicket was still a paradise. Even Hitler's pilots had been unable to conquer that . . . Then and there we resolved that cricket would go on, that Old Trafford would rise again, even nobler than of old.' Committee-men not away fighting the war met straight away and started to plan for the day of that phoenix-like emergence. Volunteers cleared the ground and repaired as much damage as they could as soon as the war ended.

And an appeal for £100,000—criticised on account of its ambitious nature and the priority need for houses and other buildings —met with a widespread and generous if not quite adequate response. Cricketers all over the cricketing world sent contributions and many gave their services for fund raising matches and functions. So did many footballers. Old Trafford's pavilion and stands rose again. Fallows, if he did sometimes fall short of perfection as a captain—as in the Roses match at Old Trafford in which he hit his career highest score, 35, but failed to declare in time to have a real chance of victory—had his moments of sheer inspiration. In the Surrey match at Old Trafford, a two-sweater affair under leaden skies, he declared at just the right moment when Lancashire had slumped to 92 for 8 in the second innings—and then, again at the right moment, put on Ikin, who was inclined to be erratic but was always liable to break up a stubborn partnership. The change worked; Ikin took several wickets but Fallows astutely brought back Bill Roberts, at that time the most consistent left-hand spinner in the counties. He had played in the 'Victory Tests' and had been hailed as a possible successor to Hedley Verity who had, to the sorrow of cricketers at all levels everywhere, been killed in the war. Again the move worked—and Lancashire won a thrilling game by twenty-seven runs. Fallows showed his flair again in the

Nottinghamshire match at Old Trafford, forcing a win by fifty-eight runs after two declarations in spite of interruptions by rain.

But it was Washbrook's year, without equivocation. In the month of July he scored 1,000 runs but, more remarkable still, he actually aggregated 1,025 with an average of 145 in only three weeks, between June 26 and July 17. As remarkable as the statistical aspect of this personal boom was the colossal stamina Cyril Washbrook was called upon to display. He made more than 100 runs in each of seven consecutive games and hit five centuries (including 109 for the Players) and much of the time in between was spent travelling. In that three weeks he covered rather more than 1,500 miles, sometimes ending his journey between matches well after midnight and once at 2 a.m., after a Lancashire bus had lost itself—in Lancashire.

After this irksome experience Washbrook opened the innings for Lancashire against Essex and, at the close of play, was 128 not out, a considerable contribution to his team's victory. Manchester was reached well after midnight and, that morning, Washbrook again opened, hitting 108 off the bowling of the Indian tourists. He suffered a severe blow in the ribs which would have kept a less tough character out of the game. But, in the second innings, he went in lower down the order and saved his side with a valiant undefeated innings. Washbrook's greatest innings, perhaps the greatest by any batsman that season, was not a century, but it turned a forlorn hope into a great bid for victory and ensured a truly dramatic finish.

At Old Trafford Essex had hit 349 and 219 for 9, at which point T. N. Pearce, who had scored 140 in that long first innings, declared. Lancashire had six wickets down for 93 runs against the Essex fast bowlers, Bailey and P. Smith. Phillipson, who had taken 7 wickets for 108 runs, then hit 51 and Ikin 81 to make the total a respectable 270. After rain on the last day Lancashire needed 290 runs to win in only 150 minutes and the Essex bowling was exceedingly hostile. Washbrook abandoned his usual solid defence to make, with Place—who also exploded a reputation for dependable rather than dashing batsmanship—an heroic bid for victory. Both hit at anything, yet Washbrook's strokes never lost their artistry. Place was, perhaps, the more impudent which was quite uncharacteristic and electrifying so far as the spectators were concerned. The pair actually hit 150 runs in 65 minutes. The great challenge failed, but only by fifteen runs with fourteen minutes to spare. Washbrook also showed his range of strokes in a delightful innings for England against India on his own ground. Oddly, he and Compton took precisely the same time to reach 50—80 minutes, which would be regarded as pretty fast scoring in a Test today. By the end of the 1946 season Jack Fallows had won an abiding place in the affections of the Old Trafford supporters. His name was familiar enough, for his own connection with the club went back many years as did his father's.

In 1947 they had to get used to a 'stranger' as his successor, Ken Cranston from Liverpool. The name had 'leaked out', which led to some resentment but, in a matter of days Cranston, through his own personality and his own evident cricketing ability, was 'accepted'. Cranston swept through first-class cricket like a tornado. After only 13 county games he was playing for England; in his second test he earned himself immortality by taking four wickets in six balls; and, on his first tour at the end of his first season he found himself captain of England because Gubby Allen was out of the first Test against the West Indies. He played once against Australia, in 1948, scoring 10 and 0 and taking 1 wicket for 79 runs and then, at the end of only his second season, he left first class cricket altogether, to practise dentistry in Liverpool and play cricket for the local club, and hockey—at which he also excelled. His departure was certainly a disappointment to Lancashire. Harry Makepeace, never a fulsome character, asserted that Cranston was the most gifted boy player he had ever coached. Between May 1947 and September 1948 for Lancashire and England he took 170 wickets with his medium pace, accurate bowling, hit more than 2,000 runs and held nearly fifty catches. Under him Lancashire were as great a team as there was in the championship. Middlesex beat them to the title but then it was the season of unfading glory for the Lord's 'heavenly twins', Denis Compton and Bill Edrich.

Lancashire, however, won a splendid last game of the season at Lord's, watched by a gratified crowd aggregating 60,000 (oh!, for a third of them today). Washbrook and Place had a wonderful season as openers. They scored 350 together against Sussex and might have beaten the record set up by MacLaren and Spooner 44 years earlier had not Cranston (properly putting the result before the record) declared the innings closed. They also put together 233 in the Sussex return match, 183 against Gloucestershire and 177 v Cambridge University.

Lancashire appeared to be just as fine a side the following year, 1948, but, no doubt partly due to the number of unfinished matches, they descended to fifth place. It was another wonderful season for Washbrook in spite of an injury which kept him out of a number of games. With this stroke of bad luck and Test match calls he was only able to play in 14 county matches yet he hit 1,391 runs and scored a century approximately every third innings. Nottinghamshire were the victims of Lancashire's most resounding triumph at Old Trafford. Notts. were all out for 45. Cranston declared with only three wickets down, Washbrook having contributed one of his centuries, and Notts were summarily dismissed a second time, Roberts having a match record of 9 wickets for 46 runs. As professional captain of an all professional side, Washbrook dominated the proceedings in the Hampshire match, hitting 200.

The Old Trafford Test petered out in a rain-ruined draw, leaving the Ashes in Australian hands, but it was by no means without incident. Compton snicked a very fast bouncer from Lindwall on to his head and had to retire for sticking plaster and a long rest. Then he returned to carry his bat for 145 quite glorious runs—just 39 fewer than he had made in another wonderful Test innings at Trent Bridge. Washbrook was 85 not out in the second innings when Yardley declared at 174 for 3. Compton and Edrich, if less dominant than the summer before, were still liable to scintillate and scintillate they did at Old Trafford, as it was ruefully recorded, 'hitting sixes all over the Stretford area'. Nigel Howard, who was to succeed Cranston as captain, hit his first century, against Derbyshire, and Cranston himself staged a spectacular farewell performance, scoring 82 to ensure a first innings lead over Kent and then making the winning hit. Tattersall, a young cricketer on the threshold of a splendid career, took 7 wickets in the same match, and Pollard, now comparatively an old stager with a fine record behind him, reached 1,000 wickets for the county. Dick Pollard, reddish-haired, burly and cheerful, like a number of other Lancashire stars played his early cricket at Bolton and drew attention to himself in the League. He bowled fast and hit hard for Westhoughton before serving Lancashire for seventeen years of zestfully undertaken toil. He displayed in his cricket not only tireless determination but obvious enjoyment so that he was immensely popular.

Dick Pollard was much missed when he ended his career with Lancashire in 1950. So hard-working was he that he was referred to

with affectionate derision as 't'owd chain horse'. As a boy he went
to Old Trafford to watch Maurice Tate and, thereafter cherished an
ambition to bowl like him. This he never quite achieved—who
did? He was quicker than medium pace but whether or not he
needed the sea fret which, it was said, rendered Tate quite lethal in
the first hour's play at Hove, (an aid unobtainable at Old Trafford)
he did not get that fizz off the pitch which turned the ball from
Tate's massive hand into a ricocheting bullet. Nevertheless, he
played in four Test matches, was one of the select few Lancashire
bowlers to exceed a thousand wickets, and he received a benefit
beaten at that time only by Washbrook's.

The small boys who swarmed into Old Trafford in rather greater
numbers then than now, pockets distended with ginger pop bottles
and other essentials, roared their approval, whatever he did. For
he was one of them, or rather he was just the kind of cricketer every
one of them would have loved to be. The Australians visited Old
Trafford three times that season and Don Bradman, on his last tour,
played in all those games. So did Pollard. In the Test and the two
county games he took ten good wickets. But it was young Malcolm
Hilton, left-hand spin bowler from Werneth, who achieved immortality in the first of the Lancashire-Australia fixtures. In his
twentieth year and his first match for the county that season he
twice took Bradman's wicket, a feat which brought him instant
fame. The second Australian match, in August, was notable for
two main reasons. It was Washbrook's benefit and that benefit left
all others far behind. The £14,000 that great Lancashire and
England opener received remains a record today, the nearest approach to it being Brian Statham's £13,047 thirteen years later. The
cricket aspect, however, is not among Cyril Washbrook's happier
memories. On a fiery wicket in sunshine after rain he was hit on
the thumb by a Lindwall express and the subsequent proceedings
interested him only as a spectator. He played no more cricket that
season. Bradman did not enforce the follow-on, a sporting gesture
Lancashire will not forget. Nor will those present forget the majestic
133 not out scored by Bradman thereafter—his last innings at Old
Trafford which was suitably, emotionally, acclaimed.

13 *The Great Spin Battle*

Nigel Howard, the new captain in 1949—he was to follow in the footsteps of A. N. Hornby and A. C. MacLaren as England's captain too (in India and Pakistan) had a somewhat difficult first season in that capacity. Lancashire lacked a bowler of real pace, Pollard having, understandably after many years of unstinted service, lost much of his sting. Moreover both Washbrook and Place were injured more than once, the batsman stepping into the breach being John Ikin, from Staffordshire where, as a schoolboy all-rounder, he had often bowled with Sydney Barnes in the late thirties. It was a singular attack. Ikin was in his teens and Barnes turned sixty when they joined forces. And the old wizard became the young tyro's mentor. He gave him unobtrusive but ceaseless encouragement, perhaps demonstrating to him a grip or a stroke between overs, suggesting how he should attack a certain batsman or deal with an unfamiliar bowler, and—always giving a word of praise when it was justified.

The war was near when Ikin joined the ground staff at Old Trafford and he had to qualify by residence. Lancashire allowed him to play as a professional with Accrington, in the Lancashire League, which gave him invaluable experience playing against sides which included such formidable experts as Learie Constantine, George Headley, Amar Nath and Amar Singh, Macaulay and Martindale. His rise, when he did make the grade, was spectacular. In April 1946 he had been regarded as no more than likely to gain a regular place in the county side. In June he was playing for England and in July was chosen for the M.C.C. winter tour.

There was an element of coincidence about his selection for the first post-war Test trial at Lord's—it caused just as much surprise as had the selection of Barnes, his Staffs. partner, by MacLaren more than forty years earlier. He was virtually unknown and had recorded no memorable success either as left-handed batsman or as a bowler of both off and leg breaks, but was regarded more as a first change than an opener. He was, in fact, a brainy bowler and a brilliant, fearless in-fielder. At that time, however, he was wanted especially as a left-handed batsman, a breed in short supply since the great days of Woolley, Mead, Hallows, Leyland and Paynter. And India, our visitors, were short of fast bowling, stronger in leg-break bowling, for the playing of which the left-hander has a peculiar advantage. At Lord's in his first Test match Ikin scored a modest 16, staying a while with Joe Hardstaff, who was undefeated with 205. He did not bowl in India's first innings but had the satisfaction of getting India's prolific opener V. M. Merchant l.b.w. in the second; and he caught both the Nawab of Pataudi and D. D. Hindlekar. An undramatic but workmanlike start. On his own (new) ground, Old Trafford in July, his contributions were again modest but not entirely negligible, 2 and 29 not out and three catches but no wickets. His Lancashire colleague, Pollard, pleased his many fans with seven match wickets and a brisk little not out innings in a match saved in the last minutes by India's last wicket pair. Ikin appeared in sixteen more Tests, emerging with a splendid batting average of 39, though his bowling record was less impressive— three wickets costing 118 runs each.

In all first class matches he hit nearly 15,000 runs and captured 278 wickets. But his fielding throughout his career was spectacular. In his first season he held more catches than any other player in England. One was spoken of with awe for long afterwards. Marshall, of Warwickshire, drove a ball hard and looked to that part of the boundary he imagined it had reached. Some seconds passed before he realised that Ikin had held the ball only yards from the bat.

By 1949 Ikin was one of the mainstays of the Lancashire side— his century at Old Trafford nearly but not quite turned the tide against Middlesex. Lancashire created something of a sensation in 1950, declaring before the season opened that they would not use the heavy roller at all and would ration watering 'in an attempt to restore the balance between bat and ball'. The slow bowlers thereafter were able to thrive, the most successful being Roy Tattersall who, concentrating on spin rather than swerve, took 163 wickets in all matches and headed the national averages. Hilton, with his left-arm slows, also had a good season and a young fast bowler named Statham provided contrast at the other end. Poor Pollard was dropped for the Yorkshire match at Bramall Lane which

Lancashire won by 14 runs after a thrilling struggle. Tattersall and Berry, on what was described as a 'horrid' pitch were full of menace. Statham, in his first Roses match, the return at Old Trafford, started as he fully intended to go on, taking three Yorkshire wickets. But the slow bowlers largely dictated matters at Old Trafford. Low scoring reached its nadir in the Sussex game, after which Jim Langridge, the Sussex captain, protested to M.C.C. that the pitch was not fit for three-day cricket.

The match had been finished in one day. Hilton and Greenwood, a young all-rounder who played soccer in the Football League, shared the twenty wickets and Tattersall, the bowler of the year, was not even called upon. Essex were then beaten by 9 wickets and this time Tattersall was the destroyer, taking twelve wickets. Washbrook proved, if anyone wanted proof, what a truly great batsman he was, with a century on this spinner's paradise. At the end of it all Lancashire shared the championship with Surrey, on the threshold of their seven-year spell at the top. The capacity of the Old Trafford wicket to help spinners was gratifying for the Lancashire players whose ranks included as formidable a band of these wily brethren as any team in England—Tattersall, Hilton, Berry and Grieves. But when the West Indians went to Old Trafford how were the biters bit! For the first time they had been granted five-day Tests, four of them, the last at Old Trafford. Immediately before that last Test the tourists had a chance to acquire local knowledge as they played Lancashire. It was Valentine (*'that li'l old friend of mine'* in the calypso) who proved the dominant spinner of them all. Without that li'l old friend of his, Ramadhin, at the other end, he took 8 wickets for 26 runs in Lancashire's first innings and 5 for 41 in the second, spinning his side to an innings victory. So it was not surprising that the England captain, Norman Yardley, decided to rely on spin in the hands of Berry, Hollies and Laker, leaving out Bedser, who became 12th man. The policy paid handsomely.

England won by 202 runs and the battle of the spinners ended in favour of Hollies and local boy Berry, beating Ramadhin and Valentine in the number of wickets taken and in the matter of their cost. Berry had the satisfaction, on his own ground, of a return more economical than that of any other bowler on either side though Valentine took more wickets. The figures of those concerned in this great spin joust are worth recalling

	FIRST INNINGS				SECOND INNINGS			
	O.	M.	R.	W.	O.	M.	R.	W.
Valentine	50	14	104	8	56	22	100	3
Ramadhin	39·2	12	90	2	42	17	77	2
Hollies	33	13	70	3	35·2	11	63	5
Berry	31·5	13	63	5	26	12	53	4

There had been a time when England were struggling for runs and, indeed, might have been routed by Valentine as had the Lancastrians on the days before. But Bailey and wicket-keeper Godfrey Evans, taking their courage in four very capable hands, boldly attacked the West Indies bowling, raising the score by 147 runs in 125 minutes between lunch and tea. Evans, with strokes worthy of a higher position in the batting order, realised a Test number 8's dream, a century, and Bailey remained undefeated, as indeed he often was, with 82. Hutton, who had been injured and had returned to help in England's recovery when Evans departed, showed how easy it is to play elegantly—one handed, even hitting a four without the help of the other. But the outstanding memory of a cricket match full of interest is of the pitch itself.

John Arlott (in *Days at the Cricket*) described its condition on the fourth day thus: 'The pitch, difficult and fiery enough previously, had now completely disintegrated in the one day which the match had now run beyond the normal county match limit of three days. I am not using an image but a precise definition when I say that the pitch now behaved *exactly* like an ash heap.' He conceded, however, that that wicket gave us the most exciting Test match played in England since the war. That poses the question—which produces the greater entertainment, the ash heap or the shirt front?

The wicket was much improved in 1951 when Lancashire slipped gently to third place. Tattersall, perhaps a trifle stale, having been summoned, with Statham, to join the injury-stricken M.C.C. team in Australia, his haul of wickets falling from 163 to 74. Statham had a satisfactory first full season but he found himself struggling for wickets as the season progressed. After playing for the Players at Lord's he bowled 75 overs in five successive matches and took only one wicket, and in the last nine games in the county programme, he took only 13. Still he headed the county averages, with Tattersall second to him. And it was for him a

wonderful summer, even if the rain didn't help his type of bowling.
Soon after his twenty-first birthday and exactly a year after his
first appearance for Lancashire, he was playing for England
against South Africa at Old Trafford—every young Lancashire
player's dream. This was a Test match full of drama. Alec Bedser,
who had Eric Rowan caught off the fourth ball of the game, was in
such form that—with Jim Laker bowling his immaculate spinners
the other end—Statham was largely a fielder.

Bedser took seven wickets, twelve in the match, and shared
with his bowling partner Laker, in a stand of 53 which England
badly needed after losing their leading batsmen on a wicket which
was probably the most vicious on the Manchester ground that
season. Hutton had been hit several times, Graveney, in his first
Test innings, had defied the demons coming from that wicket
to show his potential though he scored only 15 runs, and skipper
Freddie Brown had played a swashbuckling innings yielding 42
runs out of 52 scored while he was there, in 45 minutes.

Statham had a moment of glory in South Africa's second innings
when he knocked Waite's middle stump out of the ground with his
third ball, but it was Hutton from over the border upon whom the
limelight fell in the closing stages of a match of many moods. On
the final day the wicket had become a lot more placid but with
rain always threatening confidence in the possibility of scoring 139
runs for victory was modified. But, as Hutton and Ikin took
charge of the bowling a new, and compelling interest was aroused.
Would Hutton reach his hundredth hundred, a feat, up to then,
performed by only twelve batsmen (Compton joined the select band
a year later). Ikin, it seemed was generously leaving much of the
bowling to Hutton to help him to this glorious target and, after Ikin
was out ten minutes before lunch, so did Simpson. When the rain
descended in torrents with England needing only four runs for
victory, there was some criticism of this magnanimity. As it turned
out, play was resumed, the runs were made—but Hutton had to wait
another five days for his century of centuries.

The most significant event in the world of cricket in 1952 was
the appearance of Frank Tyson for Northamptonshire instead of
Lancashire, his native county. For four years he was the fastest
bowler in the world, and the effect upon Lancashire's championship position if he had partnered Statham can only be conjectured.
There was much disappointment among Lancashire supporters

when it was realised that such a fine bowler had been allowed to 'emigrate'.

Nigel Howard must certainly have regretted his departure, on personal as well as team grounds. In Tyson's second season for Northants, at Old Trafford he bowled the Lancashire captain twice, for 3 and 6. Lancashire finished that season of 1952 third again behind all-conquering Surrey and old rivals Yorkshire, though they won six more matches than in the year before. These successes included a devastating win, in two days, over Worcestershire at Manchester. Lancashire hit 471 for 7 wickets at a rate of $4\frac{1}{2}$ runs per over (a comfortable winning pace in modern instant cricket) to which Ikin and Edrich contributed 189 for the second wicket in 140 minutes. Essex provided the most thrilling finish, tie-ing the match in the last over after Bailey had hit a six and a two, and had then been splendidly caught by Howard, intercepting what looked certain to be the winning hit. The hero of the year was, undoubtedly, Washbrook, who, injured, hit a double century virtually single handed, against Somerset.

Not only Tyson might have played for Lancashire but, in earlier years, that very fine Surrey and England all-rounder P. G. H. Fender ('the best county captain who never captained England,' another England captain, A. E. R. Gilligan, once said to me). Indeed Fender had a trial for Lancashire, a fact which he revealed to an incredulous Tommy Higson many years later. This event took place before World War One when Fender was working in Manchester and playing for that renowned club side. After the war, which he was fortunate to survive, Percy Fender, still prominent today in the wine trade, settled down to business in London, joined Surrey and proclaimed Lancashire's loss with the fastest county century on record, 113 not out in 42 minutes.

14 *Rain And A Crisis*

Never have Lancashire cricketers suffered quite such frustration as that which afflicted them in 1953. Old Trafford more than lived up to (or down to) its reputation, often unjustified, for continual rain. Eight whole days were washed out completely and others dismally interrupted. England and Australia, as well as Lancashire, had cause to curse Manchester's meteorological record. The heroes of the Old Trafford Test were those spectators who queued for hours on the second day in spite of an early morning downpour and a dismal forecast, paid their 5s. and stuck it out to the soggy end with the inadequate assistance of sou'westers and sodden newspapers. The total length of play, in four spasms, was 90 minutes.

Those who attended on the Saturday had better luck. For the weather improved and, with this change, the match became an exciting duel on a treacherous wicket. The Australians, that day, lost seven wickets for 97 runs. Bedser had Hole (66) caught behind the wicket off his first ball, ending a stand of 173 with Neil Harvey which proved to be the best of the series. Harvey, who had been dropped by Evans at 52 two days before, was caught by Evans at 122, and the Australian innings, which had looked like reaching formidable proportions, ended at 318. The England innings, on a pitch improving slightly but not markedly, was uplifted by the graceful power of Hutton and Compton which yielded cover drives of sheer beauty by both, dazzling late cuts by Hutton, and a majestic hooked six by Compton off Davidson.

After a blank fourth day, Bailey and Simpson put on 60 runs to insure against a follow-on, then Evans, as if to atone for his two dropped catches, scored a characteristically bustling 44. He and Bedser both hit a six and then Arthur Morris had a moment of sweet revenge, bowling Bedser, who had so often claimed his wicket. Though this was virtually his only contribution (Bedser had bowled him for one in the first innings and Laker had him caught for nought in the second) he was given the honour of leading Australia in. With no result now to be expected—and it was a dolorous fact that no result had been achieved at Old Trafford for nearly fifty years, since England's victory in 'Jacker's' year, 1905— some of the Australians decided to 'have a dip', with disastrous results. At the end of that Test of endless interruptions Australia's score was 35 for 8 or, as they would put it, 8 for 35.

Bedser had been warmly congratulated upon his 100th wicket of the season by his captain, Len Hutton, who then promptly took him off in favour of Wardle, who justified this apparent ingratitude by taking 4 wickets for 7 runs in 3 overs. So Australia narrowly survived, still with the Ashes they had held for 19 years—to lose them at the Oval in the final Test, the only one to be decided that season. Lancashire, but for the weather, might have stood a chance of ousting Surrey from the second of their seven championships in succession. Apart from the hours wasted on their own ground, both the Essex and the Glamorgan games away were reduced to one day—with Lancashire well on top—and the Worcester match was swamped to 'no decision'. The Roses match at Old Trafford was drawn but some drama was afforded by Washbrook who, having retired to have his chin stitched after a blow by a Trueman express, returned to defy him with an undefeated 65 before the game ended in nobody's favour. It was a case of history repeating itself, for Washbrook, against his old foes the year before, had saved the honour of the red rose despite a damaged hand. To fill Lancashire's cup to overflowing, in the return match at Bramall Lane, Yorkshire were saved from surely inevitable defeat—by a thunderstorm.

However there were two really exciting finishes on the rain-lush Manchester ground. Hampshire were beaten by five wickets with five minutes to spare, thanks to a bold declaration by Nigel Howard when Lancashire, 214 for 5, were 149 behind. Desmond Eagar responded to this gesture, declaring the Hants second innings closed at 103 for 4 to give Lancashire 2¾ hours in which to score 253. The match was lent some distinction by the openers on either side, Washbrook and Ikin and Rogers and Gray, exceeding a hundred in partnership (the former pair twice), and by the bowling of Statham who, with the new ball in Hampshire's first innings, took 4 wickets for 6 runs in 32 deliveries. Northants won a tense struggle by one wicket, almost entirely due to the efforts of the Australian, George Tribe—who had been bowling coach to Lancashire! After two vital catches on the first day Tribe emerged from Northampton's first ever win at Old Trafford with four wickets and two top scores, 73 and 37, both not out.

In spite of Lancashire's bad luck with the weather there were some excitingly close finishes to enliven the season, for most of which that county at least looked to have a chance of winning the championship. In the first match at Old Trafford, Bob Berry, left arm bowler at number eleven hung on to deny Warwickshire what had looked a certain victory. Against Somerset Berry took 13 wickets for 124 runs, the match ending in two days, which was a long-drawn-out contest compared with the return game at Bath. This was Roy Tattersall's match. 'Tatt' took 13 wickets for 79 runs, Somerset were expelled for 59 and 79 and Lancashire, with a modest 158, won by an innings fifty-five minutes before the scheduled close of play—on the first day. For Buse, of Somerset, it was a day of utter disaster. Marner, who scored 44, hit him for 6, 2, 4 and 6 in one over. And this sorry fiasco was his benefit match.

Tatt had another great match against Notts. taking 14 wickets (9 for 40 and 5 for 33) including a hat-trick, the distinguished victims of which were Hardstaff, Stocke and Dooland. Final disappointment came at Hove, where Sussex deprived Lancashire of second place to champions Surrey. The champions had, indeed, earlier demonstrated their superiority at Old Trafford, beating Lancashire by 8 wickets, which prompted *Wisden* to surmise that this was 'possibly the champions best performance of the season.' Jack Ikin had chosen this match for his benefit. It was not a great game for that grand all-rounder.

His opening stand with Washbrook looked full of promise but, at 63, Lock (who had a memorable match with 10 wickets and 7 splendid catches) had him caught by stumper McIntyre for 25. His score in the second innings was 12 and he did not bowl. However, the benefit exceeded £7,000 putting him (at that moment of time) third only to Washbrook and Pollard. And he once more topped 1,000 runs, coming fourth in the country's batting averages.

Jack Ikin, like many another fine cricketer (the recently mentioned Arthur McIntyre of Surrey among them) was robbed by the war of what could have been his best years. Nevertheless, for Lancashire he hit 14,327 runs in 288 matches, maintaining the high average of

37·70. He also took 278 wickets at 28·79 runs each. In 18 Tests he scored 606 runs and took three somewhat costly wickets (average 118·0). Ken Grieves headed the batting averages for the first time and Statham the bowling not for the first, or the last time; he was, in fact, on his way to his unique record of coming out top for sixteen consecutive seasons. At the end of the season Nigel Howard announced that he could no longer play regularly and the Committee appointed Cyril Washbrook, an historic decision as he was Lancashire's first professional captain.

The mid-1950s were bleak years of frustration and anxiety. Frustration because Lancashire never quite fulfilled its undoubted promise between 1946 and 1960 (turning a blind eye to 1949 when they plummetted to 11th). Lancashire were joint champions once, were seven times in the first three, and three times more in the first six. The anxiety was financial. In 1954 there was general, if reluctant realisation that a state of crisis existed. The public had become obdurately apathetic after the hectic flush of post-war enthusiasm, and the weather had been as persistently interfering as an embittered in-law.

In the four years from 1954 to 1958 the situation deteriorated until the cumulative loss reached £35,646. The good old ship, so near her centenary, appeared to be foundering. Everyone went to action stations. Even the Committee, no more, no less conservative than other county committees, pocketed their collective pride and agreed that a football pool to save the ship might be worth trying— if someone would launch it.

Volunteer 'lifeboatmen' formed a crew round the county secretary and, in the winter of 1958/9, it styled itself grandly the Lancashire County Cricket Club Auxiliary Association. The rescue proved to be a slow and arduous task but determination fired by burning zeal ensured a successful salvage operation. Statistically— a modest £1,029 in 1959 rose to £8,189 in 1963. Between 1958 and 1963 the Association raised a total of £21,546 and, additionally, handed over £10,000 for building and development. The blazing enthusiasm of this band of zealots rallied support for the county side—though its performances in the early 60s were not inspiring. The deficit of the bad old days was turned into a net profit of £7,670, an enviable figure. Lancashire was saved for the trials— and the splendours—that lay ahead.

Glancing, briefly, at melancholy 1954, Cyril Washbrook, forty

that year, faced a somewhat daunting task as Lancashire's first
professional captain. He was still one of the best batsmen in
England and a cover point in the Hobbs tradition. One of his
greatest triumphs, indeed, lay ahead of him, his heroic 98, when
recalled, though 41 and a Test selector—which silenced the
noisy critics of that choice—in the Headingley Test against the
Australians in 1956. 'Washie', as he was inevitably known, was
intensely proud of the honour of captaining the side he had served
so long. He soon proved himself a firm, if benevolent disciplinarian
and a leader of massive dignity. Still, however, the old jauntiness
would flash out. He would treat the best of bowling with an
impudence few younger players would dare to display, his cap at a
defiant angle, his bat an average-destroying rapier.

That weepy wet season, so far from allowing the burden of
leadership to distract from his performance, he topped the batting
averages and hit more than 1,000 runs, as did Alan Wharton and
Geoffrey Edrich, a remarkable collective feat considering the
limitations on play. Three matches at Old Trafford were washed
out completely. Edrich, though overshadowed by his brother Bill
who had, like him, left minor county Norfolk for the big game,
going south to Middlesex, yet resembled him in the orthodox
determination of his batting and his fighting quality; he was a bul-
wark.

On a bad wicket that quality emerged strongly, and many a bad
wicket he had to play on. When the Pakistanis beat Lancashire by
6 wickets at Old Trafford, Edrich was top scorer with a most
resolute century. The Test match was, for the 'Paks', a less happy
memory, though the weather saved the day for them. Less than
eleven hours' play was possible and in that time England scored
359, those vintage stroke makers, Compton and Graveney, dominating the Pakistani bowling, and Wardle, of Yorkshire, having a
rare old spree, hitting half a century and taking 4 wickets for 19 in
Pakistan's total of 90. In the second innings Pakistani wickets
were falling (to Bedser) like the less than gentle rain from heaven
when shelter had to be sought. Wardle was the scourge of Lancashire when Yorkshire beat their ancient rivals for the first time at
Old Trafford since the war, taking 9 Lancashire wickets for only 25
runs and 3 for 60. An 18 years old Manchester born boy from
Ruthin School, R. W. Barber, left-hand batsman and leg-break
bowler showed promise, which was certainly fulfilled in his subse-

quent career with his county, Cambridge University and England
—he scored nearly 1,500 runs and took 42 wickets in 28 Tests in
the '60s.

A.D. 1954 may not have been an outstanding vintage year for
English cricket, but for one great cricketer, Jim Parks of Sussex,
it brought one of life's milestones, and its truly imperishable
moments for him were spent at Old Trafford. He had never before
played on the ground so many other cricketers rated so highly.
He subsequently joined them wholeheartedly in this matter of
esteem, asserting that the clarity of its light, the excellence of its
cricket and the character of its spectators, knowledgeable on the
game as well as delighting in it, makes it 'one of the finest grounds
in the world to play on'. He was playing for Sussex at Hove when
a message reached him that he had been picked as twelfth man for
that Old Trafford Test against Pakistan. Later, by phone, he was
told that he was in the team as Lowson, of Yorkshire, was injured.
His father, Jim Parks senior, of Sussex and England, who had
taught him the rudiments of the game in their back garden at
Haywards Heath, telephoned him from Trent Bridge where he was
coaching, with the sage advice: 'Treat it as a game of cricket, Jim.
Don't be overawed by the occasion.' Jim's first vivid impression of
Old Trafford was—the light; next, the warmth, combined with the
shrewdness, of the crowd; and, thirdly, the feeling of apprehension
inevitably experienced by a youngster on an unfamiliar ground
playing in his first Test. It left him as soon as he reached the wicket.
He scored 15, which was a respectable rather than a spectacular
maiden Test score, but he formed an affection for the Old Trafford
ground which he has held firmly ever since. For Jim Parks, the new
boy, the time spent in the rain at Manchester was worth 'hours in
the sun elsewhere'. And the experience was invaluable.

In his book *Runs in the Sun* he wrote: 'The men of Pakistan
taught me that you work in Test cricket. If you hope to "play" in
this atmosphere you will just not hit the jackpot of success.' During
many further visits to Old Trafford Jim Parks came to relish even
more the 'wonderful' light which enabled him always to follow the
flight of the ball all the way, and the humour of the crowds. His
favourite illustration of the northerner's characteristic humour
concerns his colleague, the late Jim Langridge. He was prone
to look up to the sky, particularly in moments of stress. When
Lancashire's tenacity had led to such a moment at Old Trafford

so that he cast his eyes heavenwards, someone in the crowd offered this advice: 'You'll get no help from up there, lad'.

Jim Parks had reason to remember not only the rich humour of the Lancashire fans but their capacity for generosity, even to the point of active support for those opponents who put up a good show. In 1959, a rather better vintage than 1954 for cricket as well as for wine, he hit the fastest century of the season which earned him a prize of a hundred guineas as well as the honour and glory. He was helped, as he fairly acknowledged, not only by the Old Trafford light but, practically, by the Old Trafford crowd, which was of gratifying proportions. Jim was seeing the ball 'as big as a football' even when Statham was bowling with the new one.

And it was Statham, exemplifying the grand spirit of Lancashire cricket down the years, who walked up to him and said: 'I reckon you can easily get the quickest hundred of the season.' Parks courteously replied: 'I certainly can't with you bowling,' and proceeded to prove that he could—with the enthusiastic help of the Lancashire supporters. The bid was almost frustrated when his bat broke and he had to waste time racing to the pavilion for another. Thereafter, the spectators joined in, returning the ball as it reached the boundary as if in the chase themselves. When a hefty drive sent the ball for six over the Old Trafford pavilion a spectator was seen to be sprinting at top speed to the spot where it had landed—in the car park—to return it into play in record time.

'If anyone tells you that Lancashire people are dour people who think only of themselves please refer them to me' Jim Parks wrote in appreciation. Parks had many a duel with Statham, emerging often enough with credit. Certainly he had had the advantage of 'taking' him as England wicket-keeper, but there were not many batsmen who relished facing Statham at his fastest and most accurate. Not that he could ever 'take liberties' with him and he certainly ignored the advice of a spectator to 'charge' him which, in the Sussex idiom means to go down the pitch. The spectator, a senior member, tackled him as he was going out to bat, with the suggestion: 'You know what David Sheppard would have done to him; he'd have "charged" him.' Parks replied with respect: 'I wouldn't be in David's shoes if he did attempt to do such a thing.'

15 *Record of Records*

Old Trafford, in the summer of 1955, as glorious as its predecessor had been dismal, was the scene of an innings as spectacular as any on that ground, an innings unique in the matter of successive boundaries. The South Africans, against 'Washie's' Lancashire men had lost 7 wickets compiling only 81 runs when their number seven, P. L. Winslow, proceeded resolutely to the crease. With whirlwind aggression reminiscent of the fabulous Alletson at Hove long ago, he 'carted' Jack Ikin, scoring 30 runs off one over from him, thus—4, 4, 6, 6, 4, 4, 6. His next strike was against bowler Goodwin, whose first two deliveries he despatched for 4 and 6. This added up to 40 runs off eight successive balls. His final haul amounted to 61, including 5 sixes and 6 fours, in 42 minutes.

It was, for Winslow, a felicitous season. He not only joined Bradman in the select list of cricketers who had hit 30 runs off one over from a bowler in first class cricket (the Don's victim was Tich Freeman, of Kent and England) and come to within two of the record of records—the 32 hit off Killick of Sussex by the afore-mentioned Alletson of Notts., in 1911—but he also hit his one and only first-class century. And that was in a Test match against England also at Old Trafford. Denis Compton had done his best, with 158 out of an England total of 284, a pigmy compared with the South African giant. Jackie McGlew, who had retired hurt, returned bloody but unbowed to reach an undefeated 104, Waite recorded his first Test century and Winslow his first and last, sharing in a South African record seventh wicket partnership.

England improved on their first innings effort with 381, which included an elegant May century, and South Africa, sending English hopes soaring only to nose-dive, lost 7 wickets achieving the modest target set them. Waite hit the winning boundary off Tyson in the last over but one. A splendid summer which contained at least some of the answers to the constant, anguished or angry cries for brighter cricket, ended with Surrey champions for the

fourth successive time and Lancashire joint ninth. Edrich's innings
in his benefit match against Derbyshire scarcely fell into the brighter
cricket category. He laboured for four hours to score 56 runs but,
with the help of a century by Ken Grieves and Statham's eight
match wickets, Lancashire triumphed, and the beneficiary reaped
a reasonable harvest. 'Washie', the hardy perennial, scored more
runs than any of his team, his 1,743 aggregate including a scintil-
lating 170 on his own ground against Warwickshire.

The most dramatic single moment in the cricket season of 1956
was the moment when big Jim Laker, of Surrey, having struck the
Australian wicket-keeper, Len Maddocks, on the pad had appealed
and the umpire, almost simultaneously, had raised his finger skywards. Australia were all out, the Ashes were saved, and Laker had
performed the unbelievable feat of taking 'all ten' in Australia's
second innings, following nine in their first, a match total of 19
wickets for 90 runs.

It is true that the pitch was villainous, some said more villainous
than the Headingley wicket five years later which was so severely
castigated by the Australian visitors of that year—and some home
critics too. Puffs of dust had been discernible as early in the proceedings as the first innings which was England's, aggregated 439,
and silenced those who had sourly protested against the recall of
David Sheppard (then the 'Rev.', currently the 'Bish') after only
four games of cricket that summer.

It is not true that Tony Lock, big Jim's Surrey and England
partner, bowling at the other end, at any time sought to assist him to
reach a new and almost certainly unassailable record. Test cricket
simply does not permit such soft-hearted indulgence. Lock, with
every ball he bowled, fully intended to take a wicket if he could
and so well did he bowl that he was unlucky not to gain a gratifying
share of the spoils. But that would have robbed history of one of
its more lustrous highlights.

Like Parkin, in the dear, dead days, Laker bowled most of his
overs from the Stretford end and neither the state of the wicket nor
Lock's ill-luck should be allowed to detract from his performance.
He was the greatest off-spinner of his time, and perhaps of all times,
accurate, subtle, adaptable to all conditions and any batsman,
imperturbable and blest with a classically graceful action, beautiful
to watch. And, if he did exploit the conditions, that after all, is a
tribute to his own mastery.

How many exploiters of such intelligence and penetration have there been in all Test annals? Rhodes and Verity, Grimmett, O'Reilly and just a few more. Australia's fate was really sealed when Laker took the first innings wickets of McDonald and Harvey at 48. After tea, when the Australians had struggled to 62, Lock obtained his one reward, having Burke caught. Thereafter, in 22 balls, Laker took the remaining 7 Australian wickets to return an analysis which would have had an honoured place in the history books on its own.

When Australia followed on disaster soon struck. McDonald went off with a knee injury and Harvey then hit a quite uncharacteristic full-toss from Laker into the hands of Cowdrey at silly mid-on. At the close-of-play on Friday Australia were 57 for 1. Saturday's play was limited to 45 minutes during which the Australians scored six runs and lost the wicket of Burke, caught this time off Laker. McDonald had resumed and, on Monday, with a gale blowing, he went out to the wicket once more, batting for the fourth successive day, an odd distinction indeed. He and Craig plodded to 112 for 2 at lunch time, after which the sun got to work on the damp dust —and Laker took 4 more wickets for 9 runs. Ritchie Benaud and Colin McDonald, 'getting their nuts down', fought a dour rearguard action between meals and Lock strove as mightily as did Laker to break the partnership, a determined onslaught he maintained until the last ball. At last, after tea, McDonald departed, caught at short leg after 5½ hours of brave rather than bold batting for 89 runs.

And at 5.30 p.m. came the moment of supreme glory for Big Jim. Ever an unassuming fellow, he looked slightly startled as the crowd erupted; it was some time before the tumult and the shouting died. Celebrations, that evening, were widespread and toasts numerous. There were to be heard, too, the laments of Yorkshiremen that a native with such talent should have been allowed to go south and play for one of those London teams. More in sorrow than in anger they recalled another Laker feat, at Bradford, not five miles from the place where he was born—8 wickets for 2 runs for England against the Rest.

There were other noteworthy performances at Old Trafford that season though none to bear comparison. Alan Wharton, less conspicuous in Australian than in other company with his outsize-peak cap, had the distinction of taking 137 off the tourists' bowling, for his county. He was the first Lancashire player to score a century against the Australians since another left-hander, Ernest Tyldesley, had contrived to do so 22 years earlier. In a second match against the Australians at Old Trafford, Statham took 6 wickets for 27; and it was at Manchester that summer that Statham achieved one of his three hat-tricks, against Sussex. Pullar hit his first century and bowlers Statham and Hilton held on grimly against Trueman at his fiercest to cheat Yorkshire of victory with a last wicket stand of heroic dimensions. But the most remarkable feat by Lancashire was performed against Leicestershire.

Having declared with all wickets intact, Lancashire beat their opponents by ten wickets, thus winning without the loss of a single batsman. The pair associated in this unusual record were Wharton and J. Dyson, a more than useful all-rounder who, in ten years from 1954, scored four and a half thousand runs and took 161 wickets for the county. Jackie Dyson, off-spinner once regarded as a probable successor to Place as opening bat was nicknamed 'Deep' from his versatile sporting associations. He played football for Manchester City, employing the deep centre-forward game exemplified by Don Revie, and at cricket, he fielded either at deep third man or deep long-leg.

The West Indians, not altogether unexpectedly, beat Lancashire comfortably at Old Trafford in their 1957 tour but there were some spirited performances especially by virtually unknown players for the county. W. Heys, a native of Oswaldtwistle, who was keeping wicket—he played in only 5 matches for Lancashire—hit 7 fours in a lively 46, and R. Bowman, an Oxford blue, deputising for Statham as a bowler, hit one six and 6 fours in an attractive half century (he played in only nine matches for the county and, as a bowler proved somewhat expensive).

Bowlers again, as batsmen, saved the day in the Roses match. Statham and his mate 'Tatt', defied the Yorkshire bowlers to play out time. Statham (bowler) personally disposed of Somerset, achieving figures impressive even for him—6 for 19 and 3 for 12.

The Middlesex match was spent mostly in the pavilion but, after two blank days, the players emerged and the intrepid spectators were treated to a Compton swansong of sheer delight, a century of 1947 brilliance—in his last season. Lancashire could find little cause for rejoicing in 1958 other than the fact that they finished higher in the championship table than Yorkshire, four places higher to be exact, their rivals skulking miserably at number eleven. Lancashire demonstrating this modified superiority, won their third Roses victory since the war, at Headingley, too. Once more Washbrook was the red rose thorn in the white rose flesh, turning a threatened débâcle into a dominating position.

It was the same story at Old Trafford but the determining factor there was, as so often, not 'Washie' but 'washout'. Statham and Hilton took advantage of a tricky wicket on one side, Trueman and Close on the other, the result of this fascinating foursome being a modest lead secured by the former pair in the one innings each side completed. Hilton, though less spectacular, perhaps, than other fine bowlers in Lancashire's history, in fact had a record better than most. He actually took more wickets (926) than Cecil Parkin and also scored more than 3,000 runs. He took fourteen wickets in four Test matches. He overshadowed his brother Jim who was, nevertheless, so dedicated a cricketer that it was said he taught his two-years-old son to reply 'That's out' to the demand 'How's that?'

Stories, mostly apocryphal, of bowlers' attempts to dominate umpires are many, and one still repeated over penultimate pavilion pints concerns old Reynolds, still spoken of with some awe even by those unborn when he was the multi-duties pivot of Old Trafford. In his own playing days he had appeared not only for the county, but for the United England Eleven. Playing for this side against a district 22, he was (so he related) approached by a local umpire who said to him: 'Look here, mister; I'm feeling a bit nervous. I've never umpired in a big match like this before. Reynolds comforted him. 'You'll be alright' he said. 'Don't worry, just go to the far end. I'll be opening the bowling from there and remember, I never appeal unless the batsman is out'. Oddly enough Reynolds took most of the '22s' wickets.

16 *Pullar's Year*

So far as Lancashire were concerned, and, to a lesser extent, England too, 1959 was Geoff Pullar's year. That season, with the Indians our visitors, the promise he had shown since his debut at eighteen was abundantly fulfilled. The year before his captain, Washbrook, had sent him back to the Lancashire 2nd XI, thinking that it would do him good. He was right. Pullar returned to the county side with a new determination and concentration which ensured a brilliant season and brought him 2,657 runs including eight centuries, three against Yorkshire—enough to fill any Lancastrian's cup of happiness to the full. He hit one in each of the two Roses matches and the third for the Rest against the Champion county. His first seven innings all exceeded fifty, a feat he repeated ten times more.

He started the season as batsman number 3, was picked to open for England (and became Lancashire's number 1 too) and had the distinction of becoming the first Lancashire player to score a century at Old Trafford in a Test match. He thus played a major part in England's victory by 171 runs in a Test match—much more interesting than the somewhat one-sided nature of the contestants had suggested it would be. Colin Cowdrey, captain for the first time in place of May who was ill, announced in advance that, owing to the settled weather and the fact that the following week was a Manchester holiday, he would not enforce the follow-on. This novel and sporting procedure ensured good crowds who were richly entertained not only by Pullar's hundred 'at home' but by a maiden Test century by Warwickshire's M. J. K. Smith and a third of much brilliance by India's A. A. Baig.

There was much suspense and frustration for the spectators as well as for Baig, a 20-years-old freshman at Oxford University, when the last four runs seemed to be beyond attainment. For half an hour Baig was stuck on 96, then he joined the immortals including his compatriot 'Duleep', with a century as his first Test innings.

Wharton and Grieves as well as Pullar scored more than 2,000 runs
that summer of much sunshine, and Lancashire finished fifth in
the table. But Pullar's dominance inevitably brought comparisons
with the great left-handers of the past. *Wisden,* naming him one of
the five cricketers of the year, considered that this 6 foot, 13 stone
cricketer from Swinton 'combined much of the charm and artistry
of Hallows with, at times, the pugnacity and determination characteristic of Paynter.' Statham once more headed the Lancashire
bowling but Greenhough, regarded then as the best leg break and
googly bowler in England, took nearly as many wickets and played
in two Tests, taking 5 for 35 and 2 for 31 in the second, at Lord's.
Clayton, from Mossley, proved to be not only a dependable wicket-
keeper but a useful 7 or 8 bat.

Altogether, Washbrook, when he gave up the captaincy at the
end of a good season, could take satisfaction in the fact that this
was a better all-round side than it had been when he took over.
'Washie', though immensely knowledgeable and experienced, had
not been the best of captains. Perhaps the very fact that he had so
much greater experience and seniority than any of his team
reacted against him.

He seemed somewhat remote to some of the younger players,
and not very venturesome. But perhaps the chief factor was that
lack of balance in the team he led. Certainly he was given a free
hand. He did not have to put up with interference from the
Committee—as once did the new captain of another county side
who, in his first match, received a telegram taken out to him from
the pavilion giving him instructions as to who should bowl! Nor
did captaincy interfere with his batting. He continued to concentrate
at the crease as if batting was his only preoccupation, always
looking for the shorter ball to cut, square or fine, or to hook
impassively, precisely and with undiminished vigour. Len Hutton,
who knew his true worth better, perhaps, than any other cricketer,
rated 'Washie' so high that in one of those 'All time' World XIs
in the selection of which we all love to indulge, he put him in to
open the innings with Sutcliffe, the batsmen to follow them being
Bradman and Wally Hammond.

An up and down year was 1960 in the Old Trafford and, in
particular, the Lancashire story, with some hopes fulfilled and
others dashed, some laudable feats, one victory of victories and
some disagreeable happenings. On the bright side, Lancashire

achieved the 'double' over Yorkshire for the first time since 1893,
the year of Yorkshire's first championship, which was to be their's
again. The Headingley match, won by ten wickets, was notable for
the total rout of Yorkshire by 3 o'clock on the first day, diddled out
on a dusty pitch by the leg-breaks and googlies of Greenhough and
Barber.

Geoff Pullar proceeded to demonstrate that true batsmanship
could flourish even on a spinner's wicket by hitting an imperious
century, his third in succession against the old enemy. To this day
Pullar's five hundreds in Roses matches stands as a record. And, as
he also took a 'ton' off them in a Champions v Rest game it is
scarcely surprising that he set down as his favourite hobby:
'Lambasting Yorkshire bowlers'. Vastly more exciting and entertaining was the return match at Old Trafford. Statham and Higgs,
though lacking the double-barrelled hostility of Statham and Trueman, had become a formidable complementary fast attack and
Yorkshire's capitulation gave no hint of the battle Royal to
come.

When openers Barber and Wharton had passed Yorkshire's score
unaided by later batsmen a repetition of the Headingley landslide
looked inevitable. But Trueman and Ryan now took command of
the encounter. The pair of them, plus a thunderstorm, transformed
the scene, only stumper Clayton treating the Yorkshire quickies
with something like Lancashire disdain. So the big lead, which had
seemed to be ordained, turned out to be a respectable but hardly
overwhelming 72. Statham and Higgs now bowled without mercy
and only the two Wilsons (not related) Vic, the captain and Don,
the current Test bowler, showed much Yorkshire defiance. Lancashire needed 78 runs in two hours so that few in a huge crowd—
the three days' play drew 74,000, and that was only a decade ago!—
had any misgivings about a comfortable home win for t'lads. But
what an unforgettable two hours of breath-taking, nail-biting,
oo-ing and hooray-ing there ensued.

After forty precious minutes had slipped by there were but
sixteen runs on the board, so belligerent were Trueman and Ryan.
Barber was then run out. Half an hour later, the score having crept
on to 27, Wharton was out, then Pullar, Marner and Collins.
Grieves, the 'grafter' from Sydney, alone gave the now tense
Lancashire supporters room for hope. After Clayton had joined
him the apparently extinguished flame of hope flared again. In

twenty-five minutes during which the Yorkshire bowlers injected
into their efforts all the venom of which they were capable and the
fielders ran as if pursued by demons, 29 runs were added. To
the despair (dramatically demonstrated) of the bowler concerned,
Freddie Trueman, and of Yorkshiremen everywhere, Vic Wilson,
a renowned catcher, dropped Grieves when that splendid batsman
had, largely unaided, raised the Lancashire score to 60. Still, with
only two overs left the match could surely be saved, if not now
won... Thus the Yorkshiremen fortified their morale. But—were
there ever two more dramatic overs to provide a glorious and unpredictable finish? The last but one was bowled by Ryan. Amid
much Yorkshire jubilation he had Grieves caught behind the wicket
but Clayton, whose highest score in his whole career was 84,
impudently hit ten off that penultimate over including two fours
which, if they were a trifle lucky, would not have disgraced a batsman of renown in the suspense-charged circumstances.

As Trueman strode back for his long run-up everyone could
sense that he had every intention of taking the three wickets Lancashire had left and denying them the six runs they still needed for
victory. Surely, there were flames darting from his flared nostrils as
he tossed his glossy head high and prepared to charge. The first ball
Clayton prodded away for a single; the second 'castle-d' Greenhough, the third hit Dyson on the pads and ran away sufficiently
far for two runs to be galloped. The fourth ball was blocked by
Dyson, who stood his ground until he realised that Clayton was
tearing down the pitch like an Olympic sprinter, yelling 'come
on,' Dyson belatedly responded—and was home by a whisker. The
fifth ball went off a slender portion of Clayton's bat behind the
wicket and the batsmen scampered a single. Now came the last ball
of this unforgettable game, Trueman, his lips moving in what could,
or could not, be prayer, his formidable frame hurtling towards the
crease with a terrifying irresistability, like a jet-propelled tank,
released a thunderbolt in the direction of the leg stump. It kept low
and it would have bowled most batsmen extant. But the edge of
Dyson's bat was in the way and the gods were in the mood to
propitiate only the wearers of red roses. It glanced off that edge for
four. And the multitude rose in its fervour. Clayton's part in the
most thrilling Roses victory of all had been valiant indeed, 28 and
15 not out. And Statham had played a noble part too, economically
securing nine Yorkshire wickets. The match had been set aside for

the joint benefits of Tattersall and Hilton. The pecuniary results were gratifying.

After such a drama, even stirring deeds appear to be near humdrum. For instance a masterly 150 out of 285 against Surrey by one of the heroes of that epic Roses match, Ken Grieves, and Statham's triumph in heading the national bowling averages for the second year running, with the astonishingly low figure of 10·91 runs per wicket. There was, in fact, some drama, if in a lower key, in the Old Trafford Test match in which McLean, of South Africa, had the effrontery to hit 16 in one over off Statham. Scoring 109 out of 229. South Africa having led by 264, England batsmen Pullar (175) and Cowdrey (155) effaced the memory of a feeble first innings and far outstripped its meagre total in a glorious stand of 290 for the first wicket. This dazzling defiance guaranteed a draw.

Disastrous for Lancashire was an unpredictable and unfathomable end-of-season fade-out. Four of the last six championship matches were lost, the other two drawn. This catastrophic run deposed Lancashire from the top of the championship table where they had seemed remarkedly secure, and they were lucky to finish second to Yorkshire. In spite of the efforts of Pullar, who hit more than 1,600 runs and headed the batting averages with 46·14 and of Statham, who was top of the bowling with 78 wickets costing 17·93 runs each, the next season proved a shocking one for Lancashire and a discouraging one for skipper Barber. They finished it perilously near the bottom of the table, on 13th. Another Hilton, Colin, from Atherton (Malcolm came from Chadderton) augmented the pace attack of Statham and Higgs. Two matches were played against the Australians at Old Trafford, both full of interest.

Not a single contribution to the prevalent grousing about dull cricket was to be heard. The first resulted in a win for the tourists by 4 wickets with 7 minutes to spare after exhilarating batting on both sides. The weather itself set up a Manchester record—it was brilliantly sunny all three of those May days. Lancashire scored 310 in five hours which allowed of no slouching at all. The Australians responded by keeping up a run-a-minute pace, Harvey and Burge hitting centuries and new boy O'Neill a dazzling 74 to keep a considerable crowd vastly entertained.

The second match was for Brian Statham's benefit and again the weather was fine. What a fervent concourse turned out to pay tribute to a great Lancashire player! There were 20,000 on the ground when Pullar opened the Lancashire innings with Booth, the pair delighting them by hitting 98 before Booth departed. Pullar proceeded to a glorious 165. Clayton proved himself once more invaluable in the later stages with an exuberant 63, including three 6s, and beneficiary Statham contributed a sound 16. The Aussies then set about piling up a huge score, the first by any tourists against Lancashire to exceed 500. Lawry, Simpson and O'Neill all hit uninhibited hundreds and the spectators revelled in it all. Statham, unluckily, could not bowl full out owing to a strained side. However, he had the satisfaction of claiming the distinguished wickets of Simpson and Harvey for 39 runs, and the gratification of a £13,047 benefit, second only to Washbrook's and still one of the highest in English cricket history.

The fourth Test match at Old Trafford on July 27, 28, 29, 31 and August 1 ranks as one of the most exciting and least predictable in the whole of the 'hundred years war' between England and Australia. Ray Lindwall, in *The Challenging Tests* went so far as to describe it as the best Test match he had ever seen—outside the great West Indies–Australia tie at Brisbane. With twenty minutes only left for play, Ritchie Benaud's men from Australia won it by 54 runs. Thus they won the Ashes, but only after a battle charged with tension, absorbing in its swinging fortunes. For four of the five days Australia's chief worry was how to escape defeat, not how they were going to win. Benaud won the toss and took first innings, a decision which seemed, to say the least of it, unwise when his side was all out for 190 on the second day. Statham had rejoiced the hearts of the Old Trafford crowd with 5 Australian wickets for 53 runs.

Rain, a not unfamiliar feature in the neighbourhood, had stopped play at 3.10 on the first day but thereafter the battle raged in sunshine. When England had patiently built up a first innings total of 367, labouring at times until Peter May took command of the Australian bowling to score a masterly 95—victory for England, nearly 200 ahead, looked not merely possible but highly probable. But Bill Lawry, the tall Victorian who was destined to become Australia's captain, on his first tour already showed the authority and confidence which were to dominate so many future games. Fighting back, he and Simpson put on 113 for the first wicket in Australia's second innings.

Lawry, who had been top scorer in the first innings with 74, went

on to repeat this accomplishment with 102. Wicket-keeper John
Murray, who had four victims—six in the match—caught Simpson
off Flavell for 51 and O'Neill off Statham after he had hit 67.
Alan Davidson then ensured a big total for his side by scoring 77
not out, with bowler McKenzie, putting on 98 for the last wicket.
Before this stand England had once more looked virtually certain
to win. And there was no reason to change this view when, at 3.45
that final afternoon, England, briskly chasing the 256 runs required
to win in 230 minutes, were 150 for only 1 wicket, that of local boy
Geoff Pullar. Then came the transformation. Raman Subba Row,
who had batted extremely soundly for 49, was bowled by Benaud
(how very often his wily skill turned a match) and, though Dexter
hit a lordly and glorious 76, the remains of England's batting
crumbled. Succeeding batsmen, groping feebly, seemed to be
mesmerised by Benaud's back of the hand spin. The last wicket fell
at 5.40, less than two hours after England had seemed to be coasting
home. Benaud's analysis read:

O	M	R	W
32	11	70	6

It was a totally unexpected and, for England, a bitterly disappointing result but there were few complaints in the vast crowd present.
What a feast that was for them—133,000 attended on the five days,
an Old Trafford record. The innings of Davidson and Dexter alone
were sufficiently brilliant to justify the longest journey to the
ground. And if there were slow spells, tension was maintained
virtually from first ball to last. Geoff Pullar, whose contributions
were not negligible, 63 and 26, was to remember that Australian
side with much warmth. At Old Trafford, earlier that month, for
Lancashire he had hit off their bowlers 165 (the next highest score
was 63 by Clayton) and 42, giving him an average at home against
the tourists of 74. This was a high scoring game. Replying to the
county side's 346 Australia amassed 548 for 6 wickets declared,
Bill Lawry again hitting a century (122) as did O'Neill (162) and
Simpson (103). Lancashire were 134 for 2 wickets when the run
feast ended in a draw. The dominance of the batsmen was underlined by the fact that both sides tried eight bowlers.

Unhappy from the Lancashire point of view was the manner of
Barber's relinquishing of the captaincy. He had been critical of
the Kent captain following a drawn game and the Committee had

promptly stated their disagreement. The ostensible reason for the change, however, was to enable Barber to concentrate on developing his potential as an England player and, especially, as an England bowler. It was certainly felt that he did not use himself as a bowler often enough and that to continue as captain might be detrimental to his progress. He had been, in any case a captain who seemed not to relish the position overmuch. J. F. Blackledge, a newcomer to first class cricket though he had a sturdy repuation at League and Club levels, was given the captaincy for 1962. It was hopefully supposed that he might put new life and determination into the side as an 'unknown'—just as had Burnet of Yorkshire. These hopes were not abundantly fulfilled.

To be fair, Blackledge was unlucky, suffering much from his own and other players' injuries. Barber played under him but was evidently unsettled and he eventually left the county for Warwick-shire. There were Lancashire members who felt that greater efforts should have been made to keep him at Old Trafford, if not as captain certainly as opening bat and change bowler, or even opening bowler in the right conditions. This tall, powerfully built player of so much talent had seemed to 'belong' to Lancashire if anyone ever did. He had achieved the ambition of every Manchester-born schoolboy—to play for his county while still at school. And he had shown himself a natural cricketer of vast potential. Early in his cricketing life, the Lancashire coach Stan Worthington, had said to his father: 'That one needs no help from me'. Regret at his departure from his native soil was widespread.

Lancashire showed flashes of the brilliance that was to shine forth at the end of that decade, but they were few and fleeting. In fact, the county reached the lowest rung of the championship table in its history, one from the bottom. Only two of thirty-two championship matches were won. Blackledge played in twenty-five of them, emerging with a batting average of 15·65 but with few laurels for his captaincy. It had been hoped that Ken Grieves, the very experienced senior professional (as he was before the historic decision that year to call all gentlemen and players just cricketers) would help the new skipper, but he went into business.

17 *Tall Scores—and Yawns*

Two Lancastrians who were to adorn with much success the splendid team which emerged from the crucible at least at the end of that decade, John Bond, and a young pace bowler from Todmorden named Peter Lever, had their moments of triumph. Bond hit 109 and 38 in Lancashire totals of 320 for 6 and 154 for 3, both innings declared, against Pakistan, the match being drawn as was a second against these tourists. Lever, aged 22, was said, to his gratification, to have 'brought new life to the attack', again led by Statham, who once more headed the bowling averages.

Whether or not Lord Hawke revolved in his grave, the new status of amateurs and professionals as cricketers all and equal in the site of God, the M.C.C. and even the County Committees, was not accepted without some fulminating examples of blimpery and many a sigh for the segregated past. *Wisden* pursed its lips to utter this cautious warning: 'By doing away with the amateur, cricket is in danger of losing the spirit of freedom and gaiety which the best amateur players brought to the game.'

Blackledge departed from the scene at the end of his one season as captain and Grieves was persuaded temporarily to leave business to take over this somewhat daunting post. He had a satisfactory aggregate of 1,321 runs at the end of the summer. He also had some personal successes, notably against Kent, beaten by 23 runs after two Lancashire declarations, and against the West Indies, which provided him with one of his finest feats, 97 out of 171 and 123 out of 304.

Lancashire were a good deal more assured against the West Indians than were England. At Old Trafford the West Indies piled up 501 for 6 declared, only Dexter, with 73 artistic runs, and M. J. Stewart, with a resolute 87, putting up any real resistance to Sobers and Gibbs. The most singular feature of the game was that the West Indians had to bat a second time—to score one run required for a hollow victory.

One would imagine that an uncompleted innings of 656, with 611 in reply, a triple century, a double century and two single centuries, would be satisfying enough fare for the most avid cricket fans. Yet the fourth Test match between England and Australia at Old Trafford between July 23rd and July 28th 1964 was voted by some who stuck it out the biggest bore in Test history. To be sure there were highlights to relieve the tedium of slow scoring that was hardly justified. On a wicket which looked green enough to assist even mediocre bowlers but which proved to be innocuous enough to flatter even mediocre batsmen, the mammoth scores crept up and up, with never a real prospect of victory or defeat after the second day. The slow handclap, first heard upon the first day, was employed as a protest frequently during the subsequent proceedings. The Australians, after promising great excitement with two sixes early on the first morning, completed a hardly inspiring 253 by the time stumps were drawn, for the loss of Bill Lawry, run out when 106, and Ian Redpath, bowled by Cartwright for 19. Bobby Simpson, the Australian captain, was 109 not out, which score he had increased by the end of the second day, to 265, his side's total then 570 for 4.

On the third morning, to be fair, Simpson's scoring rate accelerated startlingly, reaching a run a minute before he was caught by Parks off Price for 311, which beat Bradman's 304 at Headingley in 1934 and elevated him to the position of runner-up in the matter of Australia's highest-ever Test scores. He was second only to Sir Donald Bradman, whose other triple century on the Yorkshire ground he relished so much, 334, had been scored just thirty-four years earlier. For the statisticians there was plenty of work. On the first day Simpson, turning a ball from Dexter to fine leg, set up a new first wicket partnership record, beating the previous best, 180 by Warren Bardsley and Syd Gregory in 1909. He and Lawry took the record up to 201 before Lawry's wicket was thrown down—and Lawry's century inspired the *Manchester Evening News* to the larky headline: 'Lawry, Lawry, Hallelujah!'

On the third day a second 200 partnership was recorded. Simpson beat Ponsford's 266 at the Oval in 1934, then R. E. Foster's 287 at Sydney in 1903–4, a Test score which for so many years appeared to be unbeatable, then Bradman's 304. A new highest for Australia looked almost certain, the end of Hutton's record likely, when Simpson, in his newly aggressive mood, was caught behind the wicket. To be fair to a very fine cricketer, Bobby Simpson's 311 was marginally faster than Sir Leonard Hutton's record-breaking 364 against Bradman's Australians at the Oval in 1938.

Simpson, to the profound relief of all present, at 12.30 on the third day declared the Australian innings closed. England's innings, after a depressing start, with Edrich departing at 15, for a time brought the game to glorious life.

Dexter and Boycott played some delightful strokes even if the pace was scarcely electrifying. In fact, that evening, after Boycott had returned to the dressing room with 58 valuable runs to his credit and an appeal against the light had been made (and turned down) Dexter was subjected to barracking as Simpson had been— but with less justification in the gloomy circumstances when caution was inevitable. But there was little reason for such irritable protest on the fourth day. The first hour brought England 51 runs; Dexter and Barrington had been together 2 hours and 6 minutes when the partnership reached 100, not bad going in view of the daunting target to save the game which could not conceivably be won.

The proceedings were not without interest. Once, Dexter left the wicket, and there was some speculation as to whether, as a prospective Conservative candidate, he was on his way to greet his leader, the Prime Minister, who was among the spectators. He was, in fact, personally supervising the moving of the sight screen. When his score stood at 108, having passed his second century against Australia and his eighth in Test matches, Dexter again left the wicket, with resolute stride. Burge, at cover, had scooped up a low shot and appealed for a catch. Umpire Buller firmly rejected it and 'Lord Ted' returned to finish an innings aristocratic if rather more ponderous than was his natural way. He and Barrington had put on 246 match-saving runs and Barrington proceeded to exceed that aggregate all on his own, reaching 256 at the end of 11 hours 25 minutes at the wicket. Parks, too, was unwontedly slow, his sixty taking two hundred minutes.

England had laboured to 611 and Australia had reached 4 for 0 in their second innings when the proceedings terminated and the somewhat dispirited fifth day attendance dispersed to seek rather more excitement upon the fruit machines and darts boards of Manchester's many pubs. Had this been a 'timeless' Test how many days would have been needed to finish it? Ten? Twelve? Imagination boggles.

What a plethora of runs that Old Trafford wicket yielded when the sun shone that summer. Yorkshire, in the Roses contest, lost only 3 wickets completing 354 runs, at which point Close declared. Boycott and Taylor had scored together rather more than had Lawry and Simpson in the Test, 236 to be precise. Boycott's 131 was his third century in successive Roses matches; Taylor's 163 was one of his finest innings. Lancashire, too, scored solidly, Pullar reaching 128, half these runs in fours, before a declaration 70 runs behind, in an attempt to keep the game alive on the last day. And a sharp contrast with the last day of the Test it was. Yorkshire accepted the challenge, declared at 83 for 1 and gave Lancashire 105 minutes in which to score 154 for victory, or be blasted to defeat, an outcome Freddy Trueman wrought fiercely to achieve. He claimed 3 of the 5 wickets Lancashire lost in scoring 64 runs. But when two more wickets were down Lancashire were within 25 of their target; they had not run out of batsmen but of time. The return match was all Yorkshire's, despite imported wile in the agile shape of West Indian Sonny Ramadhin, who bowled fifty overs and took eight wickets. Ray Illingworth, who had not thought then of becoming captain of Leicestershire or England, took 4 wickets for 9 runs in 46 deliveries. Yorkshire won by an innings. It was, for Lancashire, a season best forgotten. They rose one place in the championship table—but as that ascent took them from 15th to 14th place there was no wild rejoicing. Rather there were changes.

Brian Statham was appointed captain for the following year and the Committee was strengthened—with Lancashire's permissiveness in such matters—by a Yorkshireman, left arm slow bowler Arthur Booth, top of the first class averages in 1946 and an acknowledged cricketing brain. The moves were not spectacularly successful for Lancashire once more ascended but one rung of the ladder. Statham's handling of the team and the performances of some of the young players at least gave some promise for the future. When Lancashire received Yorkshire at Old Trafford exactly half the home side's score of 214 was hit, off the hostile bowling of Trueman and Richard Hutton, by a newcomer, G. F. Knox, whose batting had hitherto been of considerable value to Northumberland. Yorkshire took the lead, with the help of Boycott's half century (how he thrived on those Roses matches) and Phil Sharpe's 60. Yorkshire were foiled by the clock, finding themselves 33 short with 5 wickets to fall at the close.

Knox never lived up to this spectacular début. This remained his highest score in first class cricket, though he had two more 'tons', 101 against Surrey the same year, and 100 against Derby in 1966. Two other young players, Harry Pilling, perhaps the smallest physically in county cricket, and Sullivan, defied Trueman in the return match, each scoring a half century, but Yorkshire won comfortably. Statham, even if he did not lead his team to glory, earned from *Wisden* the encomium: 'Brian Statham led a largely experimental side remarkably well in his first year as captain and several young cricketers, given their chance after that "purge" of the preceding close season, gave reason for optimism as to the future of the county . . . under Statham's inspired leadership a new spirit of keen endeavour was always apparent.'

This was, indeed, the foundation laying of the greatness to come. It came gradually but that 'new spirit' was manifest in growing and glowing measure as the Lancashire team gained poise, and strength through sheer enjoyment of the game, under Statham and then Bond. Devastating rather than merely decisive was the victory of the West Indies over England in 1966—with two days to spare. Only Colin Milburn, one of the most enterprising and entertaining batsmen of any era, soon to leave big cricket through the road accident which caused the loss of an eye, showed that the West Indian bowling, however venomous, could be mastered. His 94 in England's second innings was our best by far and it was made, as the late A. A. Thomson wrote afterwards, 'by courage and controlled violence'. Garfield Sobers, now widely acknowledged as the greatest all-rounder of all time, hit a majestic 161 in his side's innings-winning run pile. Lancashire, ever ready to offer fight to tourists (perhaps because of their own somewhat cosmopolitan nature) achieved a great deal more than did England against this all-conquering Caribbean contingent, Geoff Pullar exceeding Sobers' Test total by six runs in 6½ hours, so that the county headed the West Indies by one run with four wickets only lost.

Charlie Griffith, the terror of the timid (and of the not so timid often enough) was no-balled eight times in the match, having previously been 'called' nine times in the Test, for overstepping the crease. Cricket history was made in the Roses match. After play had been limited to 95 minutes on the first day and washed out

completely on the second, Yorkshire then forfeited the first innings
—the first county team ever to do so—Lancashire declared at 1 for
0, and Yorkshire won an exciting one-day game by 12 runs. Just as
crazy was another weather-dictated battle of declarations when
Sussex were the visitors. There were three declarations, by the
Sussex captain at 69 for 1 and 140 for 4, and by the Lancashire
captain at 63 for 3. Lancashire won by 7 wickets and an exciting
finish justified the tactics used to achieve it. Lancashire were to
find little comfort in the edition of *Wisden* recording the doings of
that season. Its policy, not the captaincy, was criticised in these stern
words: 'Although Lancashire climbed one position in the championship table and gained 6 victories, the 1966 season was a very disappointing one insomuch as few of the younger players showed
improvement and the lack of progressive policy behind the scenes
became more and more apparent as the season progressed.' There
were modified words of praise for Higgs '. . . again a model of per-
severing endeavour', Lever who 'showed considerable improvement', Pilling, Bond and Knox, 'sound at times' but the strictures
continued—'a lop-sided attack and lack of consistent batting are
faults Lancashire must iron out before progress can be achieved'.
And, as if to rub it in, Barber, who could have done so much for
them as an all-rounder, was named one of the 'five cricketers of
the year'—as a Warwickshire player.

18 *Return to Greatness*

The next season Statham hoisted his team up one more place, a modest rise, but the upward movement was healthy and was bound to gain momentum. Ken Higgs had now bloomed into a player of such consequence that he was one of *Wisden's* 'five'. He was a natural cricketer who was, perhaps, always destined to come to the top, though the start to his career was modest enough. Like other fine cricketers he was born in Staffordshire (which makes one wonder why that thrusting county, with its strong League and club cricket, never became first class) at Kidgrove, near Stoke-on-Trent. As a cricketer at the High Street Secondary Modern School, Tunstall, he was 'no better and no worse than the other boys'. With his strong build he developed into a seam bowler who could keep going for long spells without losing his pace or accuracy.

He played in the Staffordshire League and he might have remained there had not Jack Ikin, who had seen him bowl, suggested to Stan Worthington, the Lancashire coach, that he should go and have a look at him. Worthington was enthusiastic. 'He might develop into another Alec Bedser,' he reported. Higgs was talked into joining Lancashire by special registration but he continued to go back to Kidgrove. He had also played football for Port Vale and his home was almost within sight of the ground. Steady seam bowling by Higgs, supported by Lever and Shuttleworth, ensured a close game when the Pakistanis visited Old Trafford and beat the county by only 17 runs.

Apart from the fact that Old Trafford was more than once water-logged—the game against India in May had to be transferred to Southport, where it was evenly drawn, and Pullar's benefit match was abandoned—the season was notable chiefly for the appearance of Graham Atkinson, specially registered from Somerset, and for a new record aggregate of wickets achieved by Statham, who beat Johnny Briggs' 1,688 gathered long ago. On August 5th, 1968, Brian Statham, bowling the 16,810th over of his career, rapped

Phil Sharpe, of Yorkshire, noisily on the pad and demanded: 'How was he?' He was out. It was the last wicket Statham took in first class cricket. After that Roses encounter, drawn at the end of a typically keen struggle, Statham, to the regret not only of Lancashire supporters but of cricket lovers everywhere, retired. His final analysis was not one of his best, 1 wicket (Sharpe's) for 50 runs in 22 overs. But nine of those overs were maidens, so accurate was he still. And it had seemed, at the end of Yorkshire's first innings, that he was going to win this most important contest all on his own. Yorkshire were all out for 61, leaving them 101 runs behind Lancashire, and Statham had these figures:

Overs	Maidens	Runs	Wickets
17·5	4	34	6

It had been an absorbing occasion, with the pattern changing swiftly and frequently.

Lancashire, though weaving uncertain willows with the exception of Barry Wood, who had been born at Ossett, in Yorkshire and had played for that county before securing special qualifications for Lancashire, nevertheless built up what looked like a winning lead in all the circumstances. But Yorkshire, not for the first time, proved extremely stubborn, and, when stumps were drawn finally, had restored the game to such an unpredictable state of equality that all those present fervently wished that it could go on. With 5 wickets standing and Close still at the crease with 77 runs against his name, Yorkshire still needed 64 runs to win.

Notwithstanding other worthy performances such as the Close fight-back, it was and always will be, Statham's match. 'George' as his devoted colleagues have always known him, could not be dissuaded from retiring. He felt that it was time to go and nobody could talk him out of that decision. But, with what satisfaction could he look back upon his cricketing life. His had been a career without a blemish. He had given long, loyal and unstinted service to Lancashire and to England and he had not made a single enemy in the process. Statistically, his was an impressive record to say the very least of it. In 29 seasons, 19 summers at home, 10 winters on tour, these were his figures:

Overs	Maidens	Runs	Wickets	Average	100 wkts	5 in inns.
16,819·5	4,262	36,991	2,260	16·36	13 times	123 times

He played in more Test matches, 70, than any other Lancashire player. He had taken more wickets than any other Lancashire bowler and more for Lancashire than any other bowler in its history. He headed the Lancashire bowling averages thirteen times and the assertion that he remains the most accurate fast bowler of all time is not easily refutable. John Arlott wrote of him (in *Rothman's Jubilee History of Cricket*): 'No fast bowler in the history of cricket can have maintained such accuracy and consistency for so long, as Brian Statham.' And Richie Benaud, from extensive personal experience in the Statham-Trueman era of such splendour, said of him that he made it nearly impossible for batsmen to make strokes against him. Only Trueman, in all the annals, took more Test wickets, his 245 lifting him above Alec Bedser and all the other 'greats' since international cricket started.

But statistics form only part of the Statham story. He was, to use a regrettably neglected word, the most chivalrous of cricketers. Once, when Charlie Griffith, of the West Indies went in to bat after having administered a bumpy battering to his English predecessors at the wicket, someone suggested: 'Let him have a bouncer.' Quietly Statham replied: 'No, I'll bowl him.' Of course the ball would occasionally kick high but 'George' Statham never deliberately bowled 'beamers', nor would he attempt to intimidate tail-enders. He might have taken more wickets had he not been so admirably inflexible on this point. Even if a down-the-order batsman was making runs he would not 'let him have one', believing that he would inevitably get his wicket without resort to violence and the instillation of fear. He was, surely, the least fiery of fast bowlers from the temperamental point of view.

In many ways he contrasted with his England partner, Freddie Trueman. Never was he heard to address the fates with posturings and picturesque if direct invective; he was not one prone to the flamboyant gesture, the anguished cry for celestial assistance. Trevor Bailey recalled (in *The Greatest of My Time*) that he had only once seen him ruffled. That was at Melbourne when he had bowled brilliantly for England, taking 5 wickets for 57 runs in 28 eight ball overs. 'Justifiably,' wrote Bailey, 'he felt he had done enough to take off his boots, put on his slippers and relax with a cigarette and a glass of beer. But, alas!, England batted in such a depressingly spineless fashion that we were shot out for only 87. Brian had to bowl again the same day. He was not amused.'

This little peccadillo apart, he was, through his playing career, virtually unflappable, equable, easy-going, with a dry but never malicious wit. He was one of the most popular players on tour of his or any ther era. He would always muck in, whether his companions wanted a game of darts (at which he is above average) or golf—though he was liable to protest that he had enough exercise on the cricket field and preferred a putting course to the championship variety—or just a natter over a glass of beer. Moreover he possessed, and surely still possesses, a skill which was much relished by his touring colleagues; he would make superb pancakes.

His pancake tossing, it was observed, was as deadly accurate as his bowling. Apart from 'George', the origin of which is obscure though the name suggests geniality and dependability, he was known as 'Greyhound' for the swift grace of his running, whether up to the wicket or round the outfield, where he made 'impossible' catches look simple—to the delight of the bowlers on his side and the dismay of batsmen on the other. As a batsman he was not in the Pullar class, though that valuable England opener had in common with him two things, that he batted left handed and that they shared a last season with Lancashire. Nevertheless, Brian/George/Greyhound had some useful knocks, even if the edge did play its part; he exceeded the half century five times and hit more than five and a half thousand runs, which is more than some of us village types, fancying ourselves in the top half of the order, have done in a lifetime. No Lancashire player has ever been more generally liked, or more respected. He is now a valued member of the Lancashire C.C.C. Committee.

Geoff Pullar, at the age of 33, after 14 years with Lancashire and 28 Tests, was released by the county to go to Gloucestershire with a special qualification to play for that county in 1969. It was not, for him, the happiest of farewell seasons. He started the programme in his usual position, number one, with 39 against the Australians at Old Trafford and, after failing in the Worcester match, hit 32 and 110 off the Middlesex bowlers (he had another good innings against them in the return at Old Trafford). But he descended in the order to number four. He played in only 13 of the 28 championship matches and was placed seventh in the batting averages with a modest 22·54 compared with a career average of 35·18 and a Test average of nearly 44. Yet that season, in the opening county match against Kent, he had reached the rarely passed milestone of 20,000 runs in all first-class cricket.

Lancashire, a team on the way back to greatness, had varying fortunes in 1969. They won the John Player Sunday League cup yet were fifteenth in the County championship table with only Derbyshire and Somersetshire below them. Yorkshire, the Gillette Cup winners for the second time, beat them in the first round of that crowd-drawing competition—which Lancashire were to win for the first time the following year. In the Player's League Lancashire won 12 out of 16 fixtures, losing only three; in the championship they won only two out of 24.

However, as they were only defeated once, by Derbyshire at Blackpool in August, it must be assumed that the real cause of their misfortunes was their failure, for climatic or other reasons, to finish matches. Twenty-one county games were left drawn, or given up without a result. The weather, indeed, was the dominant factor. Of the first seven matches, five went into the records as 'No result' (the season's total in this melancholy category reached seven), the other two were drawn. In all games played by Lancashire twenty-four were drawn and still two won and one lost. This was an extraordinary record, especially when it was not seriously disputed that Lancashire had the finest fielding side in the country and, perhaps, in all its own history.

Though the weather bore the brunt of recriminations about Lancashire's low position in the championship, (115 hours out of a possible 432 were lost) the bowlers had to take their share, for lack of penetration, and the batsmen for slow scoring. Jack Bond, however, escaped criticism. The annual report included this bouquet: 'The Committee wish to pay tribute to the magnificent leadership and inspiration provided by Jack Bond. He has the happy knack of getting more than 100 per cent from his players and was re-appointed to the captaincy in early July, at which time it was decided to re-engage all members of the professional staff.'

The West Indians, many of them by now familiar enough on our grounds as county players, proved frail opponents compared with the great days when they were such very formidable opponents, in the fifties, for instance. They lost two of the rubber of three Tests, the third being drawn. In spite of the absence of Cowdrey following his Achilles operation which robbed him of cricket for a year and the England captaincy almost certainly for good (the opportunity making the man, who happened to be Ray Illingworth), Colin Milburn, after his disastrous accident, and Ken Barrington, who had retired through ill health, England piled up runs to overwhelm the West Indians in the first Test at Old Trafford. Boycott, who was enjoying one of his peaks, opened and hit 128 in England's total of 413. The fast bowlers John Snow, with 6 wickets, and Brown with 7, were too fast for the team which, so short a time before, had been (with the help of the fastest bowlers in the world then) the scourge of the cricket world.

And Sobers was, like all great cricketers at some time or another, in the doldrums. His performances, 10 and 48 and 1 wicket for 78 runs, showed little of the brilliance and dominance that had been at his command and were to be so magnificently at his command again in 1970 when he led the Rest of the World to triumph over England. Boycott was to decline, too, sinking into one of those seemingly hopeless 'out of touch' spells. Vividly do I recall those two great cricketers trying to help each other, Sobers bowling to Boycott in the nets.

Up to mid-June five games had ended in 'No result' and four had been drawn. The first match, at Old Trafford ended with the West Indies, put in by Bond, at 227 for 5, the second with Lancashire all out 195, Nottinghamshire 49 for 2. The third was one of the most dismal of all Roses matches, ending when Bond, who had chosen to bat, declared the Lancashire innings closed at 243 for 9; and the fourth was drawn when Lancashire were 81 behind Surrey with 4 wickets to fall. It was June 20 before any result was achieved. Lancashire beat Surrey, amid considerable excitement at a result being achieved, by fourteen runs. Ken Higgs had a splendid match, taking eight economical wickets. Higgs played his last game for Lancashire against Essex at Liverpool. He did not take a wicket but he could look back with satisfaction to some outstanding feats in his last season before retirement. In the drawn Kent game at Old Trafford he had (with 3 for 55 and 1 for 14) reached 1,000 wickets for his county. He joined a select band, for only nine players had previously achieved this target in Lancashire's history. His ultimate total that so-called summer was 1,033, exceeded by only eight other Lancashire bowlers, and his total in all matches was 1,165.

Higgs, like Barnes, had played for Staffordshire, his native county. But, unlike Barnes, he made Lancashire cricket his career, becoming a regular member of the side in 1958 and gaining his cap the following season. In him Brian Statham found a stalwart partner. Though not as fast—he was rated fast-medium—he was a formidable opening partner as Lancashire's opponents over ten years found. He first played for England in 1965 and in less than three years had taken 71 wickets in 15 Test matches. He was no mean tail-end batsman, emerging from the Tests and from all first class matches with averages in double figures.

19 *Bondemonium*

The finish of the Player's league championship was close. Lancashire headed Hampshire by one point only. But Lancashire, as their crowds demonstrated, had proved themselves the most exciting team in this new version of 'instant cricket'. Of sixteen matches played, twelve were won and only three lost—one of these by two runs. One was abandoned. In the Championship, in spite of their lowly position, Lancashire were, in fact, beaten only once, Derbyshire winning by 16 runs. Clive Lloyd scored 39 in each innings. In the last game of the 1969 season, against the summer's second half tourists, New Zealand, (evenly drawn) he hit 88 and 99 and headed the county's batting averages in all first class matches though he played in only ten. The weather played a major part in Lancashire's championship misfortunes for they were certainly the best fielding side in the country. Were there bonus points for fielding—and why not?—their place in the table might have been very different.

Perhaps the season's biggest disappointment was the abandoning of one Player's League match—which was against Yorkshire at Old Trafford. It was a source of much frustration for Lancashire supporters, confident of revenge for that Gillette Cup defeat. In spite of the unprecedented number of inconclusive games Harry Pilling and David Lloyd both exceeded 1,200 runs and, with such a supportng cast in the batting order as Engineer, Clive Lloyd, Barry Wood, Jack Bond, and John Sullivan (who headed both the batting and the bowling in the Player's League averages) the colossal potential of Lancashire was obvious. David Lloyd 'technically', headed the championship bowling averages—he was so listed in the Year Book—which was hard on Peter Lever who took 52 wickets in 466·3 overs compared with Lloyd's 4 in 44.

On Sunday August 30th 1970, Lancashire won the John Player Sunday League Cup for the second time in its two years' existence when they beat their ancient rivals, Yorkshire, by 7 wickets in front of 27,549 enthralled spectators. It was the sweetest possible revenge for that Gillette Cup defeat the year before and, coincidentally, ended with the same margin. The scenes when little Harry Pilling made the winning hit ensuring an unassailable lead in the League were unprecedented in the long history of Old Trafford. Nothing like them had been witnessed since England won back the Ashes at the Oval in 1953. The crowds rushed on to the pitch to mob Pilling, cheering, clapping, back-slapping, throwing hats high in the air. Then they swarmed round the pavilion, which Pilling had reached with some difficulty, roaring again and again 'Lan-ca-sheer' and 'Jackie'—who received the ovation of a lifetime when he appeared on the balcony. Harry Pilling himself said, with obvious relief: 'What a finish—I thought at one stage we might never get it over with. It was not getting the runs that worried me; I was frightened in case the spectators invaded us and we never got going again.' The ground had, in fact, rather resembled a boiling cauldron in the last few overs of that historic game. The newspapers were ecstatic. The word 'Bondemonium' was invented by the *Daily Express* which also carried the headline, significant for Sunday cricket: 'The Day Cricket Came Back from the Dead'.

It was live enough on a Saturday, come to that, the Saturday following, when Lancashire beat Sussex before a tickets-only capacity crowd at Lord's to win the Gillette Cup as well. Once more the hero was 27-years old, 5 foot 2 inches, nine stone-minus Harry Pilling. His 70 not out, which won him the Man-of-the-match award, was enthusiastically described by his captain as 'truly magnificent'. And, again, the winning hit was his. His appearance with lofty, lanky Clive Lloyd, his partner in some superb stands, was apt to provoke gusts of laughter. Pilling, scampering down the pitch, appears to be in a considerably lower gear than the long-striding, panther gliding Lloyd, the sun glinting from his spectacles at an altogether higher elevation than Pilling's cap.

In fact the pair have a wonderful understanding which makes them a formidable run-getting combination. 'I sometimes think I might be trampled on when I'm batting with Lloyd,' says Pilling with a grin. But he does not regard his lack of height as a disadvantage. Happily for cricket, Pilling decided against being a jockey—because he did not fancy 'getting up at the crack o' dawn'. There were many among Pilling's admirers who felt that summer, and still feel, that he was unlucky not to get an England cap and that Peter Lever was a trifle lucky to get one—including, I have little doubt, Lever himself, one of the most modest as well as most likeable of cricketers. If Lever had been asked in advance which he would have preferred, a Ford motor car or an England cap I do not doubt that he would have chosen the latter.

Still, it must have been a trifle galling for him, unable to bowl during the first day of his first Test match, England v The Rest of the World at the Oval for the very sound reason that England were batting all day, to learn that Tony Buss, of Sussex, had beaten him to the prize for the first bowler to reach 100 wickets in the season. Lever needed two and there was little doubt that he would have got them on the day before the Test started, when Lancashire were in the field. Buss needed five—and he took them all while Lever was sitting in the pavilion waiting for his turn to bat. Lever, fair, spare, lithe, reached the top at a pace rather more leisurely than his bowling or his running in the field. And when he heard that he had been selected to play for England in his 30th year and his tenth season with Lancashire, with typical self-effacement and humour he said: 'If they pick me for Australia they must be short.'

When he was picked, for the 1970–71 tour, there was widespread rejoicing especially fervent among the other players selected. For Peter Lever is immensely popular and his cheerful equanimity makes him what is called 'an ideal tourist'. He has, among other attributes, a picturesque turn of phrase. When Lancashire beat Hampshire at Bournemouth in the course of their triumphant progress to the John Player cup for the second time, his comment was 'We wedged 'em in'. After the team for the Oval Test was announced, a mutual friend, cricket writer Brian Chapman, sent him a telegram which read: 'Wedge 'em in and knock 'em over.' Lever replied: 'Got your telegram and did as I was told.'

At Cardiff, towards the end of the 1970 season, when Lancashire met Glamorgan—both had still a slender hope of beating Kent to the championship and this, for Lancashire, meant the goal of goals, the 'triple crown'—Lever was greeted in the most cordial manner by the supporters of both sides. Like Hendren between the wars, Lever, in the deep, will exchange a few cheerful words with the spectators. There was, upon this occasion, some mild criticism of Shuttleworth's bowling, a young Glamorgan batsman having taken a palpably unintentional knock. 'It doesn't matter whether he's a youngster or an old man—he's out there playing cricket', Lever breezily told the critics. On the last day of that match on the Cardiff Club's ground, attractive but hardly up to county standards in the matter of amenities and some parts of the playing area (though the pitch itself had plenty of runs in it) the hopes of both sides had faded, though Lancashire were still, forlornly as it proved, pinning their faith on their last fixture. The championship, which earlier it had seemed, Glamorgan would retain, then that Lancashire would snatch it from them, now appeared to be almost in the grasp of Kent, for the first time since 1913. Kent of all teams—bottom of the table as recently as July 1. Then Shuttleworth took Glamorgan's last three wickets without any addition to the overnight score and Lancashire's hopes rose again. But Glamorgan's early batsmen, in the follow-on, consolidated and the score began to mount. So it was that Jackie Bond, ever resourceful, banked on a declaration with, perhaps, a faint chance to force a result.

The lucky batsman was Peter Walker, who was virtually given a century, supported by partners, who less spectacularly but quite briskly, pushed the score along. But, so entertaining was the batting, so gay the atmosphere that it seemed to some of us 'rabbit' cricketers present that this was one of those tip-and-run affairs known in the lower cricketing strata as a 'beer match', filling the space between the premature ending of the 'real match' and opening time. News of this jolly spree quickly spread and by tea-time, abandoned because of the early close, the ground was well filled with a crowd of astonishing proportions and joyous impartiality. It was heartening to see a strong contingent of small boys, ice lollies and autograph books at the ready, spilling onto the ground. The sporting declaration duly came, Lloyd and Engineer received a warming ovation (there is a singular *rapprochement* between Glamorgan and Lancashire), the runs flowed, and the spectators cheered. But it was not to be. The fifteen overs agreed upon were reduced to the point where the target was out of reach. Down came the shutters and up came the stumps. Kent then proceeded to add to their already handsome total of bonus points and Lancashire found themselves, in their last game, against Surrey at the Oval, undisputed 'Instant cricket' champions but without real hope of anything better than second place in the championship.

In dismal weather they failed to achieve this compromise ambition. Indeed they were lucky to emerge with a draw. So, Lancashire the great and near-supreme, ended a season so rich in promise of that triple crown, third in the list below Kent and Glamorgan. But for all-round achievement, suspense and sheer entertainment they were fully entitled to be called the team of the year if not of the century. Perhaps, had it not been for Test match calls, Engineer in the first, Lever in the last, and Clive Lloyd, the most exciting player in the country to watch, whether batting, fielding or bowling, playing a star role in the Rest of the World team . . . but such speculation, understandably indulged, is idle. Sufficient it is to recall the pleasure Lancashire gave to many thousands in the process of putting new vitality into the game.

20 *Team of Teams*

What struck the discerning visitor to Old Trafford in the last year
of the 1960s and the first of the 1970s was the exuberant, pervading
zest of the Lancashire side. It was obvious every time Lancashire
took the field that here was a team to be reckoned with, a team
properly co-ordinated. There was a flowing cohesion about it, as
there is about a hair-trained rowing eight or formation ballroom
dancing team. It was, perhaps, the best balanced team in the
county's history which made it without question the most exciting
team of the new decade, and the most successful in adapting itself
to two different kinds of instant cricket threading through a busy
'conventional' county cricket programme of the old time—and
some say anachronistic—three-day variety. It always has been an
idle, if pleasantly luxurious exercise to compare present with past,
to select imaginary teams representing what we conceive to be the
best of both, and to try to put into a modern context the great
players of long ago. Idle, indeed, and ludicrous, too. The Lancashire team of the early 1970s is as much like the Lancashire team
of the early 1870s as is the latest colour TV set to the phonograph.
Just as minutes have been relentlessly and repeatedly clipped off
the time of athletic events and shots off the returns of golfers, just
as tennis has evolved from underarm to the match-dominating
power service, so has cricket altered beyond the comprehension of
those who regard it as a tranquil, changeless aspect of the English
way of life, like cabbage and croquet.

The 'disciplining' of a fielder by putting him in a place in which
he disliked fielding—a form of authority favoured by Hornby—the
thoughtless placing of poor Fred Tate by MacLaren in a fielding
position to which he was totally unfamiliar would be unthinkable
today. Fielding is a matter of precision, meticulous precision.
Fielders are not only put, strictly according to aptitude, in the place
demonstrably best suited to them, but they are placed on spots as
exact as the bowler's mark, and they are not expected to wander.

'To the half inch', Mr Cedric Rhoades, Chairman of the Lancashire County Cricket Club's Committee said to me, as we watched
those ever welcome Sothron folk from Kent, under Colin Cowdrey,
a contest fought with the utmost keenness but in an atmosphere
of unmistakeable cordiality. Mr Rhoades continued: 'The technique
of field placing has changed enormously in the last ten years. It is
a different game today. Rules have changed. The techniques of
defence far outweigh offence. And you cannot treat players as
robots. You cannot have blanket discipline in the 1970s. It has
been tried here in the past and hasn't worked. We have a fine spirit
here because all are working together—the players in the teams,
officials, staff and Committeemen.'

Buddy Oldfield typifies the unrivalled and unflagging spirit of the
modern Lancashire side, and, indeed, he contributed handsomely
to the creation of its spirit as well as its efficiency.

He is a Lancashire man by adoption—he was born in Dunkin-
field—and a zealot. He loves Old Trafford as did old Howard and
the Hornby's, Swire and the Rowleys, and hosts of others down to
the personalities associated with the ground today, 'Washie' and
'George' Statham, Secretary Wood and 'Mac' Taylor, President
Lister, Captain Bond, the man on the gate and hosts of others. It
is true that Oldfield's service with Lancashire was broken by
service in the last war and subsequently with Northamptonshire.
But Lancashire is his first and it will be his last love. He was living
near Blackpool when he joined the Old Trafford staff, so he had a
residential qualification. The youngsters did a lot of bowling in
those days, as indeed had young professionals before them since the
first pros of all—men who were hired by the landed gentry to bowl
at them, among other jobs. The system of employing ground
bowlers still, in effect, survived. 'We started at 10.30 and bowled till
lunchtime,' Buddy Oldfield recalled to me with a grin which
seemed to suggest that they weren't bad old days at all. 'An hour
for lunch and we bowled till teatime. Often, after tea we bowled.'

Oldfield's final match for Lancashire was, oddly enough, against
Northants. For Lancashire, between 1935 and 1939 he scored more
than 7,000 runs averaging nearly 36. He played in one Test match,
against the West Indies in 1939, and might have appeared in a
good many more had it not been for the war. His one Test was, in
fact, the last before the war. Oldfield scored 80 in the first innings,
19 in the second, an impressive début. In 1953, at the age of 42, he

hit 1,280 runs, averaging more than 44, appearing above such illustrious batsmen as Compton and Cowdrey in the national list. He had a spell umpiring, then returned to Old Trafford as assistant coach under Charlie Hallows, from whom he took over.

Curiously, or fortuitously, in his early days he had been coached by Hallows' great opening partner, Harry Makepeace. His former coach, Harry's predecessor, was J. T. Tyldesley. Few counties can have had such an illustrious coaching galaxy. Oldfield's recollections of Old Trafford go back more than forty years. Like so many, if not all, fine cricketers when he dips into the store the name of Wally Hammond is liable to come out. Oldfield recalls him with relish, certainly with more relish than he does Bradman, against whom he also played. 'A scoring machine,' he calls Bradman with awe. 'Watching him batting nothing much seemed to be happening. Then you suddenly realised that he had 70 or 80 runs on the board. The greatest fast bowler?' (There is no hesitation). 'Ted McDonald —the finest bowling action I have ever seen. Nobody will tell me that anyone can have a better action than him.' Better, indeed, than Lol Larwood or Bill Voce, the scourge of all the counties and of touring sides in their heyday with Nottinghamshire. And, surprisingly, Oldfield will tell you, as he told me, that the young batsmen of his day would try to get up to Larwood's end to get away from Voce: 'being a left-arm bowler if you stepped away from him the ball followed into your chest'. So, the greatest fast bowler was McDonald. But the fastest? Frank Tyson, says Oldfield. And that assertion leads inevitably again to reflection on what a pair Tyson and Statham would have made had Tyson played for the county of his birth.

From what might have been to what is. About the Lancashire team, striding so triumphantly into the '70s, he has emphatic views, to which, as that team's coach, he is fully entitled. Farokh Engineer, from Bombay, to his mind (which is quite made up) is the finest wicket-keeper in the world, a view shared by his chairman, who also agrees with his opinion about the team spirit which exists today. 'Everybody works with everybody else', he asserts. 'We are all pals together. This is the greatest team spirit I have ever seen. You can always tell. If I go into the dressing room conversation does not cease. We are all working together.'

Rhoades gives a good deal of credit to Engineer as well as to skipper Bond for the happy, and successful, state of affairs.

Engineer he has found to be: 'One of the greatest chaps to have in the dressing room or anywhere else.' What an object lesson in true integration. Engineer from India and Clive Lloyd from Guyana must forever rank among the great Lancashire cricketers in every sense, combining boundless enthusiasm and unfailing courtesy with consummate skill and artistry. Certainly they have contributed handsomely to the cohesion, the mutual esteem, which have made contemporary Lancashire the most complete team in the county's history.

John David Bond, Jack, Jackie or just Bondie, Lancashire-born, at Kearsley, educated at Bolton school, is diffident about his part in the building of this unique team spirit. They all enjoy happiness and success, he says, and they all share them. They enjoy the cricket *and* the social side.

Though no martinet, he rates physical fitness very high and advocates squash and, in particular, weight watching. He doesn't need to tell his team what to do to keep fit. They all just take the cue from him and keep themselves in peak condition.

The role of Jack Bond as exemplar was crystallised by one comparative newcomer to Lancashire's great side thus: 'When Jack Bond, at thirty-whatever-he-is runs like the clappers after every ball I think we should feel ashamed if we didn't do the same.' Jack, in fact, celebrated his 38th birthday at the start of the 1970 season, on May 6th, making him the 'Daddy' of them all, with Engineer the next most senior, six years younger. Jack Bond, small, compact, quick-moving, earned recognition and eventually something very like veneration, the hard way. He has always been a fighter. He joined the staff at Old Trafford in 1957 but had no easy route to the first XI. It was 1961 before he received his cap. After he did receive some measure of recognition, justifying his belated selection with 1,700 runs that year (when six of the team exceeded 1,000 and one, Pullar, 2,000) and more than 2,000 in 1962, ill-luck overtook him. Like Cowdrey in that unforgettable Test match against the West Indies, he had a wrist broken batting against Wesley Hall—in 1963. He played in only eleven matches that year and in only one the following season. But with typical courage and determination he fought back to re-establish himself as a valuable middle-order batsman. And so well-respected as well as obviously dedicated was he that, when Brian Statham decided to retire, he was appointed the county captain.

As always there were some who had doubts about the wisdom of the appointment and especially the capacity of the quiet little chap who had been around so long to lead a team of talented, widely differing, individuals. They were to change their minds. From the start, John Bond, striding purposefully out at the head of the team of many talents, was demonstrably the man in charge. The hour makes the man and Bond, given his chance to prove this axiom, revealed as shrewd a cricketing brain as there is in big cricket today. On the field he is more an exemplar than a stern disciplinarian. His own fielding is neat, assured, safe as t'bank, his batting, especially in a crisis, workmanlike, unspectacular but authoritative. Often has he stayed out there, staving off threatened collapse, inspiring the tail-enders to better things than they had dreamed they could produce.

A classic example of this capacity to shore up his side was his determined innings of 79 against Warwickshire towards the end of the 1970 season. Lancashire were trailing at 119 for 6 in reply to Warwickshire's 186. But Bond's tenacity ensured a substantial lead and the chance, still, to win the championship and, perhaps, the triple crown. How much is the gift of leadership, the capacity to bring out the best in every member of a side, worth in terms of runs scored, runs saved, and catches held? Imponderable, of course, but the size of this incalculable sum to Bond's credit must be considerable.

In 1969, when his brilliant captaincy took Lancashire to the John Player League championship at the first attempt, he was, in the averages, just about where he batted, in the middle. In his career he has hit more than 11,000 runs for Lancashire, with a top score of 157 and a 'best', 76 and 101 not out against Notts, which is fair enough for a number six. Off the field Jackie Bond is a good mixer wi' t'lads, a friendly family man with many interests which include table tennis, golf and a distinct liking for brass bands. He is a perpetual and peripatetic cricket ambassador, regularly visiting many clubs round his home town of Bolton and generally stimulating interest in the game he adores and adorns.

With such a team as Jack Bond has led with understanding as well as authority, setting an example in keenness and fitness which is manifest in its performances, Old Trafford has drawn through its gates supporters in numbers other counties must envy. On the occasion of a mid-week match of no particular consequence I sat among some hundreds of members in front of the pavilion facing the advertisement which always fascinates rather than influences me—it urges me to visit Chessington Zoo in distant Surrey—and contemplated the largest gathering I have seen at an 'ordinary' county match for some years now. A warm, keen, loyal Lancashire crowd, knowledgeable too. Good tempered but not minded to put up with any nonsense from the opposition, even though they applauded good batting and good fielding with admirable impartiality. A somewhat frivolous appeal would be greeted with a stern 'Give ov-er'. A happy crowd, even exuberant. Mind you, it was a rather special day, if not a very special game. 'Everyone's smiling this morning,' the man at the gate, broadly grinning himself, had greeted me. 'That's because of yesterday.' Yesterday Lancashire had beaten Yorkshire.

The last word on Old Trafford I give to one of the most dedicated of all those who have made it an essential part of their lives. 'Mac' (for MacLaren, to be sure) Taylor, the Lancashire scorer for forty years. 'Mac' is certainly proud of the fact that the scorer is in the game all the time, having to show more concentration, even, than the batsmen. 'Six hours completely concentrating every day,' says he with much satisfaction. 'Not many batsmen have to do that —or stay there that length of time.' Today, in fact, the demands on the scorer are heavier than ever. A new competition with cars as prizes requires him to record, in addition to all other details, the number of balls received by each batsman. Looking back over it all (and agreeing with Buddy Oldfield, 'I've seen some fine players in my time but the best bowler of all was Ted McDonald, though Tyson was faster'), 'Mac' asserts firmly and without fear of contradiction, at any rate in his scoring box or the pavilion bar which lies, fortuitously, upon his homeward route: 'Old Trafford is the finest ground in the world.'

Appendix

LANCASHIRE C.C.C.
OFFICIALS 1870–1970

PRESIDENTS

1873	Mark Phillips
1874–1880	A. B. Rowley
1881–1886	Sir Humphrey de Trafford, Bart.
1887–1893	Sir Humphrey Frances de Trafford
1894–1916	A. N. Hornby
1917–1918	Lord Ellesmere
1919–1920	Sir Frank Hollins, Bart.
1921–1922	Lord Derby
1923–1924	O. P. Lancashire
1925–1926	Sir Edwin Stockton
1927–1928	Lord Ashton
1929	Rev. V. F. Royle
1930–1931	Lord Derby
1932–1933	Lord Colwyn
1934–1935	Dr H. H. I. Hitchon
1936–1937	Myles N. Kenyon
1938	Lord Stanley
1939–1940	Sir Thomas Robinson
1941–1942	Sir Christopher Needham
1943–1944	Sir R. Noton Barclay
1945–1946	R. H. Spooner
1947–1948	W. Findlay
1949–1950	Sir Edward Rhodes
1951–1952	Colonel L. Green
1953–1954	T. Stone
1955–1956	Dr J. Bowling Holmes
1957–1958	The Rt. Hon. The Earl of Derby, M.C.
1959–1960	R. A. Boddington

1961–1962	Stanley Holt
1963–1964	Rev. Canon F. Paton-Williams
1965–1966	J. S. Cragg
1967	G. O. Shelmerdine
1968	J. S. Cragg
1969–	W. H. L. Lister

HON. TREASURERS

1874–1876	John Holt
1876–1879	A. H. Wolff
1879–1881	J. A. Bannerman
1881–1900	James MacLaren
1900–1909	James Horner
1910–1917	Talbot Fair
1918–1924	Sir Edwin Stockton
1925–1932	T. A. Higson
1932–1937	A. F. Stockton
1938–1945	John Boddan
1946–1948	J. C. Fallows
1949–1958	R. A. Boddington
1959–	C. R. Davies

HON. SECRETARY

1873–1906	S. H. Swire

SECRETARIES

1906–1921	T. J. Matthews
1921–1932	H. Rylance
1932–1948	R. Howard
1949–1964	C. G. Howard
1965–	J. B. Wood.

CAPTAINS

1866–1879	E. B. Rowley
1880–1891	A. N. Hornby
1892–1893	A. N. Hornby and S. M. Crosfield
1894–1896	A. C. MacLaren
1897–1898	A. N. Hornby
1899	A. C. MacLaren and G. R. Bardswell

1900–1907	A. C. MacLaren
1908–1914	A. H. Hornby
1919–1922	M. N. Kenyon
1923–1925	J. Sharp
1926–1928	Colonel L. Green
1929–1935	P. T. Eckersley
1936–1939	W. H. L. Lister
1946	J. A. Fallows
1947–1948	K. Cranston
1949–1953	N. D. Howard
1954–1959	C. Washbrook
1960–1961	R. W. Barber
1962	J. F. Blackledge
1963–1964	K. J. Grieves
1965–1967	J. B. Statham
1968–	J. D. Bond

Index